THE CHILDREN'S Bread

Receiving and Ministering God's Gift of Healing

BY

ELAINE C. BONN

McDougal Publishing is a ministry of The McDougal Foundation, Inc., a Maryland nonprofit corporation dedicated to spreading the Gospel of the Lord Jesus Christ to as many people as possible in the shortest time possible.

Published by:

McDougal Publishing

P.O. Box 3595
Hagerstown, MD 21742-3595
www.mcdougalpublishing.com

ISBN 1-58158-055-X

Printed in the United States of America
For Worldwide Distribution

Dedication

I would like to dedicate this book to my husband, **Bud,** and my children, **Kim, Terri and Steven,** who have listened dutifully and lovingly over the years to what God has spoken to me. Also to all the devoted healing teams, who have worked tirelessly in prayer for those who have come in need.

ACKNOWLEDGEMENTS

My gratitude to my Southern Baptist grandmother, Ga Ga, who prayed for my healing at age five by the laying on of hands, and imparted, not only healing into my body, but also a profound call to teach the Word of God with signs following.

I am also indebted to Rev. Jim Goll, who prophesied over me: "Elaine, write the book."

I owe a debt of gratitude to countless ministers of the Word at Rhema in Tulsa, Oklahoma, who not only taught the Word, but taught it with faith.

Last but not least, I am indebted to Pastors Jim and Ramona Rickard of Church of the Resurrection in Brooklyn Park, Minnesota, who gave me an open door to teach and minister in my call.

These have all made a significant impact on my life, and I am grateful to them.

Contents

But He [Jesus] answered and said, "It is not good to take THE CHILDREN'S BREAD and throw it to the little dogs."　　　　　　　　　　　　Matthew 15:26

INTRODUCTION

For more than thirty years now, the healing ministry has been my passion. It is a passion born out of my own need for healing, both physical and emotional. This very real need led me on a journey through the Scriptures in search of God's promises regarding healing.

As with any quest, tenacity, perseverance and stamina were required, but the effort expended brought forth abundant benefits. Not only did I receive the healing I so desperately longed for, but God put another desire in my heart — the desire to teach others what He had taught me.

In January of 1999, I fulfilled a lifelong dream by opening the Healing Rooms of Minnesota. Healing teams were established so that people could come and learn the biblical precepts on healing. Men and women were taught how to receive healing for themselves, as well as how to minister healing to others. Repeatedly, God has worked miracles in the lives of these precious ones.

Teaching classes on healing has taken me outside of Minnesota and the United States, for the truths printed within the covers of this book belong to more than just a chosen few. These precepts are meant for the entire Body of Christ. They are a vital part of the legacy left for us by Jesus, of which healing is just one part.

It is *"for such a time as this"* that I now share for the first time in printed form what I have been teaching all these years in class after class. This book encompasses the training which volunteers receive prior to becoming part of the ministry of the Healing Rooms of Minnesota.

Jesus paid such an incredible price to purchase abundant life for us that I long to see as many people as possible have the joy of walking in the good health and perfect wholeness that He has provided. This is my prayer for you as you begin to read these pages.

You, too, are about to embark on a journey. What you will encounter along the way will be biblically based, but you will also find plenty of real-life stories and practical applications that you can incorporate into your own personal life. This is a journey meant for all those who are hungry for what God has to offer, and I trust that you are among them. If so, may you receive a goodly portion of *The Children's Bread,* and may you then go out and use it to feed others who are also hungry.

Elaine Bonn
Minneapolis, Minnesota

CHAPTER ONE

THE BIBLICAL BASIS FOR HEALING IN THE TWENTY-FIRST CENTURY

My people are destroyed for lack of knowledge.

Hosea 4:6

Far too many of God's people among our current generations have indeed been destroyed for lack of knowledge, and this has been just as true in regard to our physical healing as it has been with any other aspect of our Christian experience. This is a tragedy, because God's will for the physical healing of His children is absolute and is made very clear to us in His Word. To remedy this situation, we must learn the truths of His Word concerning healing for ourselves, and then we must teach them to others.

Many of us have learned enough about the salvation of our souls that the enemy can no longer deceive us in this regard. With healing, however, it seems to be a totally different matter. There is much confusion on this issue among twenty-first-century Christians and much lack of clarity. I am convinced that this is because we have not been taught the full truth about this aspect of Jesus' sacrifice for us.

Many of us grew up in traditional churches where these things were not taught. Personally, I am descended from six generations of ministers, but our church never taught us that healing was part of the atonement. We were taught that God *could* heal us (if it happened to be His will), but that's as far as it went. It was only when I began to come into the things of the Spirit that the Word of God became alive to me and I began to realize how much we had missed by not being taught this fuller aspect of God's salvation.

Even after I was part of a "Word" church, where people were memorizing and quoting the Scriptures, I found that many still did not fully believe what they were confessing. It is in knowing the promises of God and in believing them that we receive. Let us, therefore, begin by laying a solid biblical foundation for the healing ministry in the twenty-first century.

IN THE BEGINNING

In Genesis 1, we have the account of the Creation. Those of us who believe the Bible believe that God made everything, and I read there in the pages of Genesis that everything He made was *"good"* (for example, Genesis 1:4, 10 and 12). Tell me, then: On which of the six days of Creation did God create sickness?

I've looked for the answer to this question, as have others, and I don't find it anywhere in the biblical record. On none of the days of Creation did God decide to make sickness. His creations were all *"good,"* and sickness certainly doesn't fall into that category.

Then, if God didn't create sickness, and sickness is not part of His original plan, where did it come from? The answer is that sickness came into the world because of sin. Sickness is part of the curse that came upon man for his disobedience to God, and it came into the picture only when death made its ugly appearance. Sickness is the forerunner of death. It never was God's will, and it never will be.

James declared a further truth about our Creator God

and His goodness that helps us to understand that sickness is not from Him:

> *Every good gift and every perfect gift is from above, and comes down from the Father of lights, with whom there is no variation or shadow of turning.*   James 1:17

Everything that comes from God is *"good,"* and with God, there's no varying, no *"variation"*; there's no *"shadow of turning."* This means that once God has said something, He never changes His mind. He means it. His promises are just as good today as they were thousands of years ago. Like Him, they never change. Sickness, therefore, is clearly not from God. It came into the world because of sin, and is part of the curse.

Still, when sin came into the world, with all of its terrible consequences, God already had a plan to save mankind from its vile effects. He had prepared His Son before the worlds were formed to deliver man from the curse of sin. In the fullness of time, Jesus would come to earth and live, and then He would take our sin upon His own body on Calvary's cross.

Once Jesus had completed this act of atonement, things would then revert to God's original plan (for those who believed and received). We could then go back in time and experience a restoration of all things that were lost in the Fall. We would suddenly became part of the greatest recovery program the world has ever known, a free program for anyone who cares to believe in Jesus.

The important question about all of this is not, "Is it so?" The question is, "Will you believe that it is so?" Everything God did was for you and me; everything He did was *"good"*; everything was created as He wanted it. We also were created in the way He wanted us. And, believe me, He didn't

11

create us sick or maimed or limited; He created us whole and well. Sickness came when sin entered the picture.

SIN CAME INTO THE WORLD, AND WITH IT, SICKNESS

Wherefore, as by one man sin entered into the world, and death by sin; and so death passed upon all men, for that all have sinned.   Romans 5:12, KJV

First sin entered the world, and then death followed. When sin came, death came with it, and sickness, a precursor of death, was part of that curse. When *"death passed upon all men,"* it was only then that men began to experience sickness. This was all the result of sin. Because of sin, death came, and because of sin, sickness came.

Sin and sickness affect much more than our bodies. We have sick souls, sick marriages, sick homes and sick cities and nations — all because of sin, and the goal of the enemy is to lead us all into death — spiritual and physical.

As a result of the Fall, mankind is sick. Men and women have sick minds, sick families, sick pocketbooks and sick businesses. If we fail to take back what has been stolen from us, our end is assured. The world is destined for sickness and death, but it need not be so with those who believe in Jesus.

God's plan is for our full restoration. He not only desires our physical healing; He wants us to have healthy marriages, healthy homes, healthy finances and healthy businesses.

Jesus already paid the price for all of this to be accomplished, and the only thing remaining for us to do is believe and receive, to accept the gift. If we don't grab hold of it, it will pass us by.

Sickness and disease are simply death in its early stages. John recorded Jesus' words that explained it all very clearly:

> *The thief cometh not, but for to steal, and to kill, and to destroy: I am come that they might have life, and that they might have it more abundantly.* John 10:10, KJV

So when we see forces that steal and kill and destroy, we can know that they are not of God. That's all the work of the enemy. Would we ever describe Jesus as a thief? Would we ever think that He is a destroyer? Certainly not. He came that we *"might have life"* and that we might have it *"more abundantly."* Sickness is clearly not of God.

We who know Christ are destined not only to have eternal life in Heaven, but also to have *"life more abundantly"* down here. This is God's will for us today, and it is possible because of the sacrifice Jesus made on Calvary's cross. Peter wrote to the churches:

> *... who Himself bore our sins in His own body on the tree, that we, having died to sins, might live for righteousness — by whose stripes you were healed.*
>
> 1 Peter 2:24

Jesus took upon Himself our sin and gave us His righteousness in exchange. All we have to do is receive it. And, in the same way, Peter added, *"by [His] stripes you were healed."* Healing was part of the provision of Jesus, because He dealt with sin and its consequences.

> *For He made Him who knew no sin to be sin for us, that we might become the righteousness of God in Him.*
>
> 2 Corinthians 5:21

THE CHILDREN'S BREAD

Along with our sin, God laid upon Christ our sicknesses. He bore them for us, and we are healed through His sacrifice, just as we are saved through His sacrifice.

HEALING IS PART OF OUR REDEMPTION

Physical healing is, then, clearly part of our redemption. This word *redeem* means "to fulfill as with an oath or a promise; to deliver; to reclaim." Jesus is our Deliverer. He has reclaimed us. He did for us what we could not do for ourselves, because we had sinned. And through His sacrifice, we are redeemed.

Another meaning of the word *redeem* is "to regain possession of by paying a price; specifically, to recover." We were lost to God through the Fall of man, and we had lost His blessings, including health and healing. But we have been redeemed. God reclaimed possession of us through the sacrifice of His Son Jesus.

Redeem also means "to recover, to pay off; to receive back; to satisfy; to set free; to rescue; to ransom; to rescue from sin and the penalty of sin." Oh, thank God, we're redeemed, and part of our redemption is the promise of renewed physical health.

Some might argue that the body has nothing to do with our redemption, that redemption is only spiritual, but if that were true, we would have no hope of the coming resurrection of our bodies. Redemption is for the whole man.

As Christians, we sing about redemption, we pray about it and we rejoice in it, but far too often we understand very little about exactly what it involves. We have been redeemed by the blood of the Lamb (most of us do understand that fact). God chose to give us our redemption in this way because life is in the blood. Jesus gave His blood for us, and when He did, He was offering us His very life.

We have been bought and paid for by the precious blood of Jesus Christ, and there's power in His blood. When we accept Him as our personal Savior, we receive a Holy Ghost blood transfusion. And from that time forward, we have His life in us.

The Scriptures declare that life is in the blood. When Jesus was crucified and His blood flowed out, that was the symbol of life. He did that for us, and we can now lay claim to the benefits of it. Understand your legal rights, get mad at the devil for what he had done to rob you of your blessing, and start taking back what is rightfully yours.

Blood has always been precious to the Jewish people, and the most precious blood of all was shed for you and me. After His death, Jesus went into the presence of the Father and sprinkled that blood, His precious blood, on the Mercy Seat of Heaven. When He did this, the Father accepted it and marked our sins "PAID IN FULL." Then Jesus sat down at the Father's right hand to be our Advocate. Now, when we sin, we have someone to plead our case. What could be more wonderful?

JESUS BECAME A CURSE FOR US
AND PROVIDED OUR ATONEMENT

Christ has redeemed us from the curse of the law, having become a curse for us (for it is written, "Cursed is everyone who hangs on a tree").		Galatians 3:13

Through His sacrifice, Jesus took us out of the hands of the enemy and put us back into the hands of Almighty God. He paid off our debt, and we were returned to our original owner. Jesus thus dealt with sin for all those who will receive it. He said:

"For God so loved the world that He gave His only begotten Son, that whoever believes in Him should not perish but have everlasting life."   John 3:16

This sacrifice was for *"whoever,"* and any man or woman can lay claim to it. It represents the greatest act of love known to mankind:

"Greater love has no one than this, than to lay down one's life for his friends."   John 15:13

The sacrifice of Jesus on the cross of Calvary was accepted by the Father as full payment, full payoff, for our sins, and we could never have achieved that for ourselves. He set us free, and that freedom is available to every one of us.

Being free is now a choice, an act of our wills, and healing is part of that freedom. We are saved from sin because we make a conscious decision to accept Jesus as our personal Savior, and the same is true with healing. Being healed, or physically redeemed, or saved, also demands an act of our wills. We must believe it and receive it.

Our God is the Healer, and healing is part of His complete atonement package. *Atonement* means "satisfaction for a wrong; the redemptive work of Christ." What Jesus did brought reconciliation between God and man, reconciliation for you and me. All those who desire to be healed and those who desire to be used in a healing ministry must understand this truth.

An atonement is a substitution, something given on our behalf. Christ was our atonement, our substitute. Our sins can be washed away, and we can become sinless before the Father only because Jesus was, indeed, our atonement. In the same way, we can be healed because Jesus died in our place, and we are no longer under the curse of sin. Most of us have no problem believing that Christ's atonement includes the forgiveness for our sins, but many still struggle with healing as part of the atonement. Why is that? It's part of the same wonderful package.

HEALING IN OLD TESTAMENT TIMES

Healing was available in Old Testament times. David, for instance, sang these beautifully inspired words:

Bless the LORD, O my soul;
And all that is within me, bless His holy name!
Bless the LORD, O my soul,
And forget not all of His benefits;
Who forgives all your iniquities,
WHO HEALS ALL YOUR DISEASES,
Who redeems your life from destruction,
Who crowns you with lovingkindness and tender mercies,
Who satisfies your mouth with good things,
So that your youth is renewed like the eagle's.

Psalm 103:1-5

No biblical statements could be more powerful. He *"forgives all [my] iniquities"* and He *"heals all [my] diseases"!* What greater proof could we ask for concerning God's will and healing?

Isaiah foretold an ever greater time to come, through the Messiah, the Anointed One:

Surely He has borne our griefs
And carried our sorrows;
Yet we esteemed Him stricken,

17

The Children's Bread

Smitten by God, and afflicted.
But He was wounded for our transgressions,
He was bruised for our iniquities;
The chastisement for our peace was upon Him,
AND BY HIS STRIPES WE ARE HEALED.

Isaiah 53:4-5

This passage was quoted several times in the New Testament, and we can all claim it as our own: *"By His stripes we are healed."* God said it, I believe it, and that settles it.

God further revealed His will concerning healing in the Old Testament when He showed us His names. They are all wonderful and speak of His power and His willingness to display that power on behalf of His children.

He is Jehovah-Jireh, the Lord our Provider (see Genesis 22:14). He is Jehovah-Nissi, the Lord our Banner (see Exodus 17:15). He is Jehovah-Ra'ah, the Lord our Shepherd (see Psalm 23:1). He is Jehovah-Shalom, the Lord our Peace (see Judges 6:24). He is Jehovah-Shammah, the Lord Who Is Present (see Ezekiel 48:35). And He is Jehovah-Tsidkenu, The Lord our Righteousness (see Jeremiah 23:6). But He is also Jehovah-Rapha, THE LORD OUR HEALER. He said to His people:

> *"If thou wilt diligently hearken to the voice of the LORD thy God, and wilt do that which is right in his sight, and wilt give ear to his commandments, and keep all his statutes, I will put none of these diseases upon thee, which I have brought upon the Egyptians: for I am THE LORD THAT HEALETH THEE."* Exodus 15:26, KJV

Jesus Was Both Sinless and "Sickless"

Jesus, as Life itself, was an example to us all while He was living on the earth in flesh (as a man). During that time,

18

He never got sick. There is no record of His ever having developed even as much as a headache. He never had a bad day, and the reason is clear. Jesus was sinless, and therefore the curse of sin (sickness included) had no place in Him. This meant He was also "sickless."

I'm not suggesting that everyone who experiences sickness has sinned in some way. As we have seen, sin has passed upon all men, and with it, the curse of sin. As Christians, we are redeemed from the curse, and that should free us from sickness as well. Many of us still suffer sickness, however, and I am convinced that it is because we have not yet realized what is ours through Christ. When our sins were forgiven, the curse of sin was broken from our lives. We are now the righteousness of God, and the righteousness of God is *"good."*

We have been fully redeemed from the curse. Jesus finished the work, and it included healing for our bodies. He set an example for us while He was here on earth. He didn't live in constant sickness and pain. He rejoiced in perfect health. This is remarkable for many reasons.

Jesus was a man on the go. He had things to do and a limited time in which to accomplish them. His schedule was full, and He often spent long nights in prayer.

This, of course, was His secret. He knew how to get alone with His Father in prayer, how to renew Himself and how to cast aside heavy weights that could have done harm to both His spirit and His body. He stayed well because He had no fear, no worry and no sin.

And because Jesus had no sin, He had no sickness either. Then God's will for us is clear. We are redeemed, freed from the penalty of sin, and that includes our healing.

Healing in the Ministry of Jesus

From the very beginning of His ministry on earth, healing was a great part of what Jesus did, and many of the gospel accounts refer to miraculous healings. Matthew, for instance, recorded:

> *And Jesus went about all Galilee, teaching in their syna-*
> *gogues, preaching the gospel of the kingdom, and heal-*
> *ing all kinds of sickness and all kinds of disease among*
> *the people.* Matthew 4:23

> *Then Jesus went about all the cities and villages, teach-*
> *ing in their synagogues, preaching the gospel of the king-*
> *dom, and healing every sickness and every disease among*
> *the people.* Matthew 9:35

In one such healing, that of a leper, Jesus expressed His will concerning healing:

> *When He had come down from the mountain, great*
> *multitudes followed Him. And behold, a leper came and*
> *worshiped Him, saying, "Lord, if You are willing, You*
> *can make me clean."*
> *Then Jesus put out His hand and touched him, saying,*
> *"I am willing; be cleansed." Immediately his leprosy was*
> *cleansed.* Matthew 8:1-3

"I am willing." It was never a question of whether or not healing was God's will or whether or not Jesus believed in it or practiced it. It was God's will, Jesus believed in it, and He practiced it everywhere He went.

The amazing thing about this particular incident and others like it was that they took place before the cross of Calvary. How much more true then is it today that God's will is to heal the sick among His people. We are the redeemed of the Lord, redeemed through Calvary, redeemed in every way.

This leper was not "saved" in the Christian sense of the word, and if Jesus was willing to minister to him and heal him, how much more will He be willing to minister healing to those who believe and are part of the covenant for which He paid such a high price. God definitely wants to heal the sick today. There can be no question about that fact.

A NEW TESTAMENT HEALING MINISTRY
FOR "THOSE WHO BELIEVE"

Jesus, after having healing as a great part of His own ministry on earth, left an important commission with His disciples when He was about to leave and go back to His Father:

> *"Go into all the world and preach the gospel to every creature. He who believes and is baptized will be saved; but he who does not believe will be condemned. And these signs will follow those who believe: In My name they will cast out demons; they will speak with new tongues; they will take up serpents; and if they drink anything deadly, it will by no means hurt them; they will lay hands on the sick, and they will recover."*   Mark 16:15-18

What does this word *"saved"* really mean? In a general sense, we consider being saved to include only salvation from sin, but it means much more. The salvation provided for us by Jesus' death and resurrection includes our physical healing as well. God's salvation is a complete package deal, and includes deliverance and subsequent freedom from every oppression. When we, by faith, receive the Lord

Jesus Christ as our personal Lord and Savior, we receive much more than we could have anticipated. So healing is ours as part of Jesus' free gift of salvation to all mankind, and healing is also part of our ministry to the world. It is among the *"signs"* He said would follow us when we believe.

Although many of the Bible books speak of signs, John's writings are particularly notable in this regard. God wants to give us evidence of His presence with us. This evidence, that the Bible calls *"signs,"* is not just for our personal knowledge, but also for the sake of others to whom we speak about our Lord. Such signs will only follow those who believe for them, and they can only be done in the name of Jesus.

One of the signs that will follow when we go forth in the name of Jesus and in faith is the casting out of demons. We call this deliverance, and deliverance and healing go together. We cannot be completely healed without deliverance, and we cannot have complete deliverance without being healed. Those who are healed are delivered, and those who are totally delivered are also healed. Again, this ministry is available to *"those who believe."*

We will also *"speak with new tongues."* If we encounter serpents, they will not harm us. If we accidentally drink anything deadly, it also will not harm us. Then comes the glorious promise: *"They will lay hands on the sick, and they will recover."* These are not the words of a mere man, but the words of Jesus. Our Lord Himself said that we would lay hands on the sick. And He declared (with no hesitancy), *"They will recover."* We must believe it, and begin to act on it.

Who can have this ministry? Is it just for those who are part of the fivefold ministry — apostles, prophets, evangelists, pastors and teachers? That clearly cannot be the case, because Jesus said, *"These signs will follow those who believe."* That would include every member of the Body of Christ. None of us is excluded, and each of us is called to this ministry of physical restoration of the sick and suffering through the laying on of our hands.

In reality, many of the healing lines we see around the country are unnecessary. If each of us would minister healing to those around us, as the Lord desires, we would have much less need of standing in such lines. God has called us to share His power and to show His love in this way. "Would you pray for me?" therefore, is a question we should each be eager and ready to respond to. This is our joy; this is our privilege in the Lord.

When we lay hands on the sick, we can stand on the promises of the Word of God and expect the sick to recover. God said they would (*"They WILL recover"*), so it's a sure thing.

Not everyone recovers instantly, of course. Healing, for the most part, comes forth over time. But we believe, whether we see the healing instantly or not, and God brings it to pass in His own time.

The Proof

After Jesus had spoken those final words to His disciples and was received back into Heaven, a wonderful thing happened, and Mark recorded it:

> *So then, after the Lord had spoken to them, He was received up into heaven, and sat down at the right hand of God. And they went out and preached everywhere, the Lord working with them and confirming the word through the accompanying signs. Amen.*
>
> Mark 16:19-20

As Jesus' ministry on the earth was ending, the ministry of His disciples was just beginning. The disciples were now doing the same things Jesus had done, because He was working through them. He had told them to preach and to bring healing and deliverance to the people who received their message, and they immediately went out and began to test what He had said.

What happened when the disciples obeyed the command of Jesus? Wonder of wonders, what Jesus had said worked! Healing miracles began to come. They were just as simple as He had said, and they were just as sure as He had said.

This, then, is the ministry to which God is calling you and me today. The early disciples went out and preached the goodness of God everywhere, and we must do the same. They had the Lord working with them, and we need His presence, too. They saw the Lord confirming the Word they preached with signs, and that is also what will convince our world today.

"These signs will follow THOSE WHO BELIEVE." That's you and me, and it's time to start demonstrating this truth to the men and women around us.

"I PRAY THAT YOU MAY ... BE IN HEALTH"

The apostle John wrote to the early churches:

Beloved, I pray that you may prosper in all things and be in health, just as your soul prospers.   3 John 2

But this is not the word of John; it is the Word of God. Who wants us to prosper? Of course, John wanted the early believers to prosper, but this is God speaking, and He is saying that *He* wants you and me to prosper and be in health.

Prosperity speaks of much more than money, and that is clear in this passage. He said, *"I pray that you may prosper IN ALL THINGS."* But we can only prosper in other ways as our souls prosper.

Being *"in health"* is part of God's desire for our prosperity. So, if we are sick, He wants us to be healed. The fact that He compares our physical health and our spiritual health is an indicator of just how important this is to God. Would anyone doubt that He wants our souls to prosper? Surely not. So the fact that we are to prosper and be in health *"just as [the] soul prospers"* reveals His will in this regard.

Although it is true that Christians need more inner healing than physical healing, that doesn't minimize God's desire for our physical health. And when we are healed in the spirit, that often translates into better health in the body.

The Conclusion

So, sickness was not God's will for us from the beginning. It was a result of sin, and Jesus has dealt with sin and its consequences through His sacrifice on Calvary. Healing, then, is part of the atonement paid for our complete freedom from bondage. Healing was available in the Old Testament, but its manifestation accelerated in the New Testament, when Jesus healed all who came to Him and left a command with His disciples to continue bringing healing to those who would believe the message they preached. God's will is clearly expressed throughout the Scriptures. He wants us to prosper and be in health. These are firm foundations on which we can build the healing ministry.

THE CHILDREN'S BREAD

THE IMPORTANCE OF LAYING THIS BIBLICAL FOUNDATION

We cannot exaggerate the importance of laying such biblical foundations for healing for ourselves and for those to whom we minister. Such foundations are the basis of all our beliefs and subsequent actions in this matter.

Jesus knew the importance of God's Word in all things. Just after He had been baptized in the River Jordan, He went into the wilderness to fast and prepare for His ministry (see Luke 4). There He stayed, fasting and praying, for the next forty days. Until that fortieth day, the devil had not even attempted to turn Jesus aside from His appointed task. Now, however, he knew that Jesus was in a weakened condition, and in that moment, Satan chose to attack.

This tactic is not unknown to most anointed believers. Satan does the very same thing to us, attacking us when we are tired, hungry and irritable, when we are facing the most serious problems of our lives, when our jobs are not working out right, when we have had a lousy day, when we have had a fight with our spouse, and when our children are acting like they belong to someone else. This is one of the enemy's favorite tactics.

When this happens, what should we do? Well, what did Jesus do? He didn't try to argue with the devil. He didn't say, "Do you know who I am? Do you know that I was present in the beginning? Do you know that I emptied Myself of all that I was and all that I had to come to earth for such a time as this?" No, He simply said, *"It is written,"* (Luke 4:4), and that was enough to defeat the devil.

Satan did not give up entirely, of course. He came back several more times during Jesus' wilderness experience, and every time he came back, he had a new tactic, a new temptation. Still, Jesus didn't change His answer. To each temptation, to each attempt to subvert Him, Jesus answered, *"It is written"* (Luke 4:8 and 10). That was enough, and that's what you and I need to do, too.

Why was Jesus' method so powerful? Because God's Word is anointed, and the devil knows it. The more you and I speak those anointed words, the more they will become part of our spirits, and the more easily they will do their work.

The truths about healing are settled, and when people come to our Healing Rooms for prayer, there is no question about what God wants to do for them. Their healing has been paid for on Calvary. There can be no ifs, ands or buts about this issue. We can tell the devil where to go (in the name of Jesus) and to take his sickness with him, because the work has already been accomplished.

It is time that we get angry about the deception the enemy has perpetrated on the Body of Christ. This explains why so many are sick. We are living far below our privileges because we have not yet been awakened to our true potential. We seem to be living somewhere in the Old Testament. It's time that we recognize the benefits of Calvary and begin to enjoy them.

IGNORANCE IS NOT BLISS

When we know something is available, we can claim it. So, in this case, ignorance is certainly not bliss, and keeping us in the dark is one of the favorite tricks of the enemy. Each of us needs to go where we can hear the Word of God preached in its fullness, and we need to spend time in the Word for ourselves. Its promises are powerful to set us free.

The enemy will never stop harassing us, but he also knows his limitations. Even if he cannot harm us, he will continue to threaten. He will do all that we permit him to do. Take authority over him and break his hold on your life — in the name of Jesus. Stand on God's promises.

In our training sessions, I repeat some of these truths over and over again because they are the basis upon which we minister healing. Therefore, we want all those who will minister in the Healing Rooms to get them rooted deep inside their spirits. If you will do the same, you will be healed and you will be able to bring healing to many others.

Every church should be teaching healing, just as much as any other part of our salvation. Healing is just as important as the forgiveness of sins, for instance. And every church should teach and practice deliverance.

Because we have emphasized certain teachings over others, we have received certain blessings and not others. And because we have not been well taught concerning healing in the atonement, far too many of God's children are sick.

Healing is received in the same way salvation is received. If God said it, I believe it, and that settles it. All those who believe and receive salvation should believe and receive healing also. It's just that simple.

Now, let us take a look at our authority for the healing ministry.

CHAPTER TWO

AUTHORITY FOR THE HEALING MINISTRY TODAY

Then some of the itinerant Jewish exorcists took it upon
themselves to call the name of the Lord Jesus over those
who had evil spirits, saying, "We exorcise you by the
Jesus whom Paul preaches." Also there were seven sons
of Sceva, a Jewish chief priest, who did so.
And the evil spirit answered and said, "Jesus I know,
and Paul I know; but who are you?"
Then the man in whom the evil spirit was leaped on them,
overpowered them, and prevailed against them, so that
they fled out of that house naked and wounded.

Acts 19:13-16

If we do not have authority to heal, or if we are not sure
that we have authority to heal, Satan will surely know it,
and he will be slow to obey us. When we lay hands on those
who are sick and suffering, we must recognize that they
are afflicted by the enemy, and we must know that we have
authority to change their situation. Satan knows when we
have it and when we don't, and we can't fool him.

What does this word *authority* mean? It is "the right to
command and enforce obedience." When we have authority, we have the right to act officially. We can command and

expect our commands to be obeyed. Authority is personal power.

Authority, however, is always delegated power. The authority you have is derived from, or delegated by, another. In our case, His name is Jesus. He is the Great Physician, and we are His servants for bringing healing to the world.

AUTHORITY IS DELEGATED

When a policemen on the street takes some action, he is not acting on his own. Rather, he is acting on behalf of his chief, who has given him authority to do certain things. A school teacher has authority over her pupils, an authority given to her by a school principal or by the local board of education. The pastor of a church has authority, but it comes from a local board of trustees, from a congregation as a whole, and, hopefully, from God.

Authority is never unlimited. A policeman can do many things, but not everything. A teacher has specific guidelines to control the extent of her authority, and each pastor has certain limitations. God has given us authority to act on His behalf, accomplishing certain specific assigned tasks. We never have all authority for everything, but we do have authority for the tasks He has assigned to us.

Most of us have not yet accepted or exercised our God-given authority. Often, we have even failed to realize that we have such an authority. A lack of authority or a lack of exercising of our existing authority has held us back from accomplishing much more for God.

Our Father is now calling us to stand up, put on the full armor that He has provided for us and go forth to do what He has called us to do. The Lord of Glory has authorized us to do it, and because of that, nothing can hinder us — except fear or lack of movement on our part.

We are always waiting for God to do something more, when He has done all that He needed to do. The rest is up to us. The authority has been given; now we must accept it and put it to work. Stop waiting for God to do something, and start doing what He has already called you to do.

Sometimes false pride gets in our way. After receiving powerful words from the Lord about what we can do, we hang back, insisting that we cannot yet do these things. This allows the enemy to "walk all over" us. It is time to put him in his place and take our authority in God.

AUTHORITY REQUIRES SUBMISSION

Those who walk in authority have learned to walk in obedience to a higher power. Jesus said:

"If you love Me, keep My commandments."
John 14:15

Later, He said it in a little different way:

"If you keep My commandments, you will abide in My love, just as I have kept My Father's commandments and abide in His love."   John 15:10

So Jesus gave us more than a command; He gave us a divine example. We are to love and obey our heavenly Father, just as He did.

Some have the idea that submission to a higher power somehow represents loss. This is just the opposite of the truth. Obedience always brings blessing, a measure of increase. God showed us through Moses that a whole litany of blessings would come upon those who were obedient to Him and a whole litany of curses would come upon those who were not (see Deuteronomy 28). If we walk before God in obedience, blessings will pursue us and overtake us. We won't have to keep looking over our shoulders to see if something good is coming. God's favor will surely catch up with us. He is always ready to increase His people.

So we want to be obedient to God, and we want to use Jesus as our example. I encourage those I teach about the healing ministry to underline the following passage in their Bibles:

> *Then Jesus answered and said to them, "Most assuredly, I say to you, the Son can do nothing of Himself, but what He sees the Father do; for whatever He does, the Son also does in like manner. For the Father loves the Son, and shows Him all things that He Himself does; and He will show Him greater works than these, that you may marvel."*   John 5:19-20

This is a very important passage for those who have a desire to enter into a healing ministry. If Jesus could *"do nothing of Himself,"* how much more it is true of us. We must remain attached to the Vine, Jesus, just as He remained connected to His Father. Jesus is the Vine, and we are the branches, and as long as we stay connected to Him, we will bear much fruit. Our connection is maintained through obedience, through doing what God has called us to do.

Because our authority to heal is based on our submission to the Lord, if we are walking in rebellion, we will struggle to bless others and ultimately not succeed.

OUR AUTHORITY IS BASED ON A COVENANT

Our authority is based on a faith covenant with the Lord Jesus Christ. In the beginning, God made a covenant with the first man, and later He made other covenants with other men. Then, in the time of Jeremiah, He spoke of what He called *"a new covenant":*

> *"Behold, the days are coming, says the LORD, when I will make a new covenant with the house of Israel and with the house of Judah — not according to the covenant that I made with their fathers in the day that I took them by the hand to lead them out of the land of Egypt, My covenant which they broke, though I was a husband to them, says the LORD. But this is the covenant that I will make with the house of Israel after those days, says the LORD: I will put My law in their minds, and write it on their heart; and I will be their God, and they shall be My people."* Jeremiah 31:31-33

We have a wonderful new covenant written within our hearts. It is a lasting covenant that works by mutual consent. As long as we remain attached to our Lord, Satan has no power over us. All authority outlined in this covenant is ours.

Not long after He began His ministry, Jesus declared in the synagogue in Nazareth:

> *This day is this scripture fulfilled in your ears.* Luke 4:21, KJV

What was Jesus saying? He had just finished reading a long quote from the book of Isaiah that prophesied the coming of an Anointed One who would set God's people free from their bondages and heal all their sicknesses. He was saying that He was the fulfillment of the promise spoken of in times past of a new covenant.

Now, we are the inheritors of this new covenant.

33

THE CHILDREN'S BREAD

Through Jesus, the Mediator of this covenant, we have received authority to continue the ministry He began on the earth. He is our authority. He made the provision for man's restoration, and then He commissioned us to spread that Good News and to administer the covenant, and that includes physical healing. There could be no greater authority.

THE SPIRIT BRINGS AUTHORITY

When the Holy Spirit came upon Jesus' disciples after His departure, He provided them with an enduement of power, or authority, to act on Jesus' behalf. He also enabled them to perform the works Jesus had performed during His short years of earthly ministry. This enduement of power through the Holy Spirit is what makes our covenant different from all others. The former covenants were little more than types and shadows of what was to come. This new covenant is the standard God has set up for all eternity for those who belong to Him.

The crowning covenant of the Old Testament was the Law, which came into effect during the time of Moses. But the Law only reminded men of how far they had come short of God's perfect will. Try as they might, the people of the Law could never measure up to its demands. They were always looking forward to some better time, and that better time came when Jesus was born into the world.

Our covenant with God is now complete, because it depends on the goodness of Jesus, not on our own goodness. Consequently, those who are in Christ have a unique power and authority. This quickly became evident in the lives of Jesus' humble co-workers:

> *Then he called His twelve disciples together and gave them power and authority over all demons, and to cure*

*diseases. He sent them to preach the kingdom of God
and to heal the sick.*   Luke 9:1-2

We, as inheritors of the promise, have these same rights
and privileges. We are called by God and empowered by
God to act on His behalf. He has given us authority to
preach His Word, to command demons and to bring healing to those who are sick — *"To cure diseases,"* and *"to heal
the sick."* Wow! That's powerful!

This same authority is available to us today. We have
been granted authority to establish the Kingdom of God in
the hearts of men everywhere, and healing clearly plays
an important role in this work.

Exercising Your Authority
Does Not Always Come Easily

The early believers fulfilled their calling, but not without suffering some inconveniences:

*Therefore those who were scattered went everywhere
preaching the word.*   Acts 8:4

Because of persecution, the believers in Jerusalem were
forced to scatter, but that didn't stop them from fulfilling
their divine calling. They now preached *"everywhere,"* and
you can be sure that they also cast out demons and brought
healing to the sick — as Jesus had commanded them to do.
The dispersion of the early believers was meant by Satan
for harm, but God used it for good. If it had not been for
their dispersion, the Church would not have grown as rap-
idly as it did.

The problems the disciples experienced on a daily basis
during that time probably did not feel like blessings to

them. They may have been wondering why the bottom seemed to be falling out of everything, why things were so difficult. But God knows how to bless us far beyond our wildest dreams. Blessings will come — although not always in the way we expect them.

When we know the examples of God's Word, we have nothing to fear. The great stories of the Bible can carry us through any trial. These truths were recorded for our benefit, for our understanding and enlightenment. When we see what God did for the men and women of the Old Testament, especially, we can rejoice, for we have a better covenant. In that covenant, our God-given authority is fulfilled. In that covenant, we find grace, mercy and the enduement of power from the Holy Spirit for our lives.

Jesus was conceived by the Holy Spirit, and when we receive Him, that same miracle takes place in us. We become new creatures. We need this renewed conception so that we can be part of the new covenant, from which we derive our authority. It is given by Jesus:

> *"Behold, I give you authority* [I give you divine power, I give you enablement] *to trample on serpents and scorpions, and over all the power of the enemy, and nothing shall by any means hurt you."*   Luke 10:19

How wonderful! God has delegated authority to us. Know that it exists and that it is for you today.

Since we don't often encounter serpents and scorpions in our everyday lives, what do serpents and scorpions represent to us in this passage? They represent the principalities and spiritual powers we will surely face. But don't worry. God has given us authority over them all. They cannot do us any harm, because we stand in the authority given to us in Jesus' name.

Authority for the Healing Ministry Today

"Do Not Touch My Anointed Ones"

God warned the people of the Old Testament:

"Do not touch My anointed ones,
And do My prophets no harm."   1 Chronicles 16:22

Why? Because God will avenge His servants. They are His representatives. They stand in His power and act under authority from Him. God has given you dominion. Possess it and begin to walk in it.

This doesn't mean that it will come automatically. In his letter to the churches, Jude showed us that we must *"contend"* for what is ours:

Contend earnestly for the faith which was once for all
delivered to the saints.   Jude 3

Contend for it. Strive for it. Fight for it. It's worth every effort you may put forth. Then, once you have possessed it, stand in it.

Stand Firm in Your Anointing

The enemy tries to frighten us. Peter admonished:

Be sober, be vigilant; because your adversary the devil
walks about like a roaring lion, seeking whom he may
devour.   1 Peter 5:8

It is important to know that our enemy is not a lion; he just tries to act like one. He's more like a paper tiger. He makes a lot of noise and stirs up a lot of confusion, but if we know our authority and stand strong in it, he is always

37

forced to back down. Put on your full armor, get into position and know that you can defeat this foe. God has called you, and with that call comes authority.

We must, however, be vigilant. The weakest army is said to be one that has just enjoyed a victory. When we are too confident, we become most vulnerable. We feel able to "kick back," and that's when the enemy knows to come after us. When you have had a victory, that's the time to dig in. That's the time to pray more. That's when you need time alone with the Lord. Get ready for the next battle. If we are on guard and contending for authority, Satan will not catch us unawares. Authority comes from God, and as long as we stand with Him, Satan can do us no harm.

JESUS' AUTHORITY QUESTIONED

At one point, John questioned Jesus' authority:

Now it came to pass, when Jesus finished commanding His twelve disciples, that He departed from there to teach and to preach in their cities.

And when John had heard in prison about the works of Christ, he sent two of his disciples and said to Him, "Are You the Coming One, or do we look for another?"

Jesus answered and said to them, "Go and tell John the things which you hear and see: The blind see and the lame walk; the lepers are cleansed and the deaf hear; the dead are raised up and the poor have the gospel preached to them. And blessed is he who is not offended because of Me." Matthew 11:1-6

What good news this was! These servants could go back to John and tell him that Jesus had authority because of the works He was doing. This is the same authority the

Lord has given to us to do His works in our time, and our works declare our authority.

After Jesus was baptized and came up out of the water, a dove appeared and landed on Him. This was part of His preparation. Then He had to go into the wilderness for additional preparation. You and I, too, must go through periods of preparation, but we can know that great power and authority awaits us. It's only a matter of time and perseverance.

Lose Your Fear of Satan

Once we have faced the enemy and seen that we have power over him, we lose the fear of him, and it is not so difficult to face him the next time. The first time I rode a roller coaster, I was terrified. I was sure I was about to die and wondered how I had allowed our friends to talk me into doing something so utterly foolish. I was the most relieved person when the ride came to a stop and I was still in one piece.

But when I realized that I had all my parts together and was safely on solid ground, suddenly it came to me how much fun the ride had been, and I wanted to go again. I wasn't afraid anymore. Before it was over, I had ridden the roller coaster about a dozen times, until all the thrill was gone out of it and it was no longer a challenge.

The first time we do something, we are often afraid, but after we have done it enough, we can "do it blindfolded." That's what the anointing gained through preparation will do for you. God is preparing us so that we will not be intimidated every time we face the enemy. As we learn more and more about this foe, we realize that we are more powerful than he is through Jesus, and we can overcome him.

How do we overcome? The Scriptures tell us:

THE CHILDREN'S BREAD

But those who wait on the LORD
Shall renew their strength;
They shall mount up with wings like eagles,
They shall run and not be weary,
They shall walk and not faint.   Isaiah 40:31

I trust that you are one of *"those who wait on the LORD."* It is there, in His presence, that we receive our authority.

"AS THE FATHER HAS SENT ME"

Although He had been conceived by the Holy Spirit, Jesus didn't go out to minister until He had received the Holy Spirit and His anointing. He had come in the form of a man, so He had to take this step to reveal to us the way to be anointed. Afterward, He gave us a commission:

So Jesus said to them [the disciples] again, "Peace to you!
As the Father has sent Me, I also send you." And when
He had said this, He breathed on them, and said to them,
"Receive the Holy Spirit."   John 20:21-22

This is our commissioning: *"As the Father has sent Me, I also send you,"* and it represents the delegation of power and authority to us. God the Father sent Jesus, and Jesus sends you and me. So, do we have authority? Who could doubt it, when we have been commissioned by the Lord Himself?

We have the Lord's Great Commission. We are to *"go."* We are to go in the name of Jesus. And as we go, signs will follow us. One of those signs, again, is that sick people will be healed. We have full authority for the healing ministry.

Because the Great Commission is not directed only to pastors and teachers or others of the fivefold ministry, but to every believer in the Body of Christ, our Healing Rooms are staffed by people from all walks of life. They are men and women who are taking up the positions to which they were commissioned by our Lord. And just as the original disciples had results as they obeyed His commission, so do those who obey Him today.

When we go somewhere for God and speak His words, we should expect signs to follow us too. This is God's way of showing that His Word is real and valid for today. This is our authority.

WITNESSES "TO" HIM

"But you shall receive power when the Holy Spirit has come upon you; and you shall be witnesses to Me in Jerusalem, and in all Judea and Samaria, and to the end of the earth." Acts 1:8

We are witnesses *"to"* our Lord. This shows our submission to Him. He's the Head of the Body, and we, as individual members, get our marching orders from Him. Whatever He tell us, that's what we are to do. He left a command for His followers when He went back to Heaven to wait for power (authority) to do the job :

And being assembled together with them, He commanded them not to depart from Jerusalem, but to wait for the Promise of the Father, "which," He said, "you have heard from Me." Acts 1:4

This *"Promise of the Father"* was the infilling of the Holy Spirit, the power (authority) from on high. This is what enabled the disciples to become witnesses *"to"* Him.

THE CHILDREN'S BREAD

GOD'S WORD IN US GIVES US AUTHORITY

Jesus said:

> *"If you abide in Me, and My words abide in you, you will ask what you desire, and it shall be done for you."*
> John 15:7

As we keep the Word of God in our hearts (and you have to know it to keep it there), we can ask what we want (*"what you desire"*) and it will be done. This is a wonderful promise that represents great authority!

One night, many years ago, I woke up in the middle of the night and sat straight up in the bed. As I did, I heard God speaking these words. *"If you abide in Me, and My words abide in you, you will ask what you desire, and it shall be done for you."* At that moment, this became a very personal promise for me, and the Lord has been working it out in my life ever since.

Each year that passes, I am able to believe a little more, trust a little more, and each year I see what God planted in me that night growing. There is still much room for growth, but God is working in me, as I'm sure He will continue to do so until I meet Him face-to-face.

AUTHORITY REQUIRES HUMILITY

Jesus taught us to pray:

> *Your kingdom come.*
> *Your will be done*
> *On earth as it is in heaven.* Matthew 6:10

Walking in authority clearly requires humility. That's

difficult for some, but Jesus showed us the way. He humbled Himself and came to earth as a man, so that we could become like Him. He had it all, but He gave it all up. He was sinless, yet He took our sin upon Himself.

Jesus chose humility, and we must too. We must humble ourselves before those who come into our healing rooms for ministry or before those we encounter anywhere in life. Many of them are such desperate, hurting individuals. They have received terrible reports, and we must feel their pain. We must love them as Jesus loves them.

We often feel very inadequate in this regard, but the Lord will help us. Humble yourselves, and God will lift you up.

BE BOLD

Our authority is a legal right paid for at Calvary, so we have every legal right to lay hands on the sick and expect them to recover. We have every legal right to command the devil to take his hands off of God's property and to expect it to happen. We have every legal right to speak the Word of God and to expect to see healing spring forth as a result.

The curse has been broken, and God has provided for our lives and for our ministries. If you are working for God, go forth in your authority and expect things to happen, and they will. Do what the Father has told you to do, and He will do the rest. This knowledge gives us a new boldness.

His Word declares:

> *Let us therefore come boldly to the throne of grace, that we may obtain mercy and find grace to help in time of need.* Hebrews 4:16

We can come boldly. Why? Because we know who we

are. We have no reason to approach God timidly. We have no reason to tiptoe into His presence. We can go boldly in, just like a child in need.

When a child needs something, does that child come timidly with a formal request? No! Children usually don't care where we are or what we're doing. They come barging in, and they are not timid about saying what they need or want.

Having desperate needs often makes us more bold. When we're truly in need, we don't sit and think about what we need to ask God, and we don't practice to get the wording right. We just blurt it out, and those bold, desperate prayers get results.

Be bold in your ministry of healing, for you have the Father's authority to act in His name.

AUTHORITY REFLECTS MATURITY

Authority is a sign of maturity, but some of us are slow to accept it because some authority figure in our past has misused the position of authority. We're afraid we might rub someone the wrong way if we get too enthusiastic, too bold. We need to get delivered from that attitude because God has not given us a spirit of fear:

> *For God has not given us a spirit of fear, but of power and of love and of a sound mind.*   2 Timothy 1:7

> *There is no fear in love; but perfect love casts out fear, because fear involves torment. But he who fears has not been made perfect in love.*   1 John 4:18

Get rid of your fears, and come boldly before God's throne.

44

Faith Reveals Authority

Any act of faith on our part is an indication that we are learning to submit to authority and walking in it. Acting in faith shows the world that we have received something, that we know what we have and that we have no fear of using it.

People are strange in that they are sometimes afraid of confident people. But when you know God's Word and you are speaking His Word, you don't have to worry about what others think or say.

Be sure of what you believe, and know the power of it, and before long, people will be chasing after you to pray for them. There are many desperate people in the world, and when desperate men and women know that you have the authority to go to the throne room of God on their behalf, they will seek you out.

"Neither Male nor Female"

When God is on your side, when He is in you and working through you, there will be no question about your authority. This is true for women as well as for men. In the anointing, there is *"neither male nor female."*

I believe in order and submission. I fully submit to the authority of the Lord, and I fully submit to the authority of my husband. If Bud feels that I should not do something, I don't do it. I may sometimes try to persuade him otherwise, but if he remains firm in his opinion, I submit to his decision. By submitting to authority myself, I can assure that I will have authority in my own life and ministry. My submission is my protection.

There is a great need in the Body of Christ for men and

women to recognize authority and submit to it. This is a sign of maturity.

As a woman, there are places where I'm still not welcomed to speak. When I *am* welcomed, I go with the full support and prayer backing of my husband. When I minister, he sits in the audience and listens, like everyone else. He has no desire for the ministry I have because that's not his calling. He is content to do what God has called him to do and to allow me to do what God has called me to do. I support him in his ministry, and he supports me in mine.

Far too many women today have risen up in rebellion against God's appointed authority figures. Let God do the work for you. He will lift you up.

In the event that someone questions your authority because you're a woman, let the Lord deal with it. If you take an argumentative approach, the only thing you will accomplish is to anger people and make a big "mess" of things. Ask the Lord to remove the scales from the eyes of those who feel that women cannot be used by Him. You can't force others to accept you. It is God who gives authority, and sometimes it takes time for others to recognize that authority. So be patient, and let Him work it out.

THE SOURCE OF MOSES' BOLDNESS

When God sent Moses to deliver the children of Israel from bondage in Egypt, he asked God whom he should say had sent him. God answered:

> *"I AM WHO I AM." ... "Thus you shall say to the children of Israel, 'I AM has sent me to you.'"* Exodus 3:14

Those are the words of a person who knows his authority. He doesn't downplay his importance and try not to sound too proud about the matter. Why is it that some people are nervous about hearing someone say, "God told me to do such and such." We should be declaring for all to hear, "God told me to do it, so the devil had better watch out, because I'm not backing down. I'm going through with this thing."

Many members of the Body of Christ are much too timid. They think it doesn't sound humble to speak boldly, but God has called us to boldness. He has made Himself available to us. And He is the Answer. He is the Healer. He's the Supplier. He is our Salvation. He's the mighty Provider. He's our Sanctification. He's our Righteousness. He's our Deliverer. When He called Himself "I AM," He meant that He was all of those things and more.

Jesus taught:

> " 'For to everyone who has, more will be given, and he will have an abundance; but from him who does not have, even what he has will be taken away.' "   Matthew 25:29

We have a modern saying that summarizes well this teaching. We say, "Use it, or lose it." If God has given you something, use it. If you don't, you'll lose it. This includes authority.

If you use what you have, I guarantee that it will be multiplied back to you. Whatever you sow, you will reap. So, never back down.

Paul wrote to the Galatian believers:

> And let us not grow weary while doing good, for in due season we shall reap if we do not lose heart. Therefore, as we have opportunity, let us do good to all, especially to those who are of the household of faith.
>
> Galatians 6:9-10

Don't quit. Don't get weary. Don't get discouraged. The harvest is coming. We *"shall reap."* Boldly stand on that promise.

If you are feeling tired or discouraged, ask others to pray with you. Then stand in your authority and expect to see the harvest.

A REEMERGENCE OF AUTHORITY

As we move further into revival, we will see a reemergence of authority. This will spark a mass movement of previously unsaved into the Kingdom. It will take signs and wonders to bring in these lost ones, so we need to pray and believe toward that end. Ask the Lord to make your hands healing hands. Ask Him to make you a miracle worker for His glory. Ask Him to show forth signs and wonders in your life as the seal of His presence with you and of your authority to act on His behalf.

When Jesus sent those servants back to John, He told them to declare what they had *"seen and heard."* It is not carnal to speak of what God is doing in your life, of how many people have been healed. It is not showmanship to point out spectacular miracles that God is performing through the laying on of your hands. In fact, this is necessary to build up people's faith. But it is also a seal of your authority.

Recently I was speaking at an Aglow meeting, and a lady stood and testified that the last time I had spoken for them, her son and his wife had received a miracle the same day I prayed for them. A few days after this second meeting, I received a letter in the mail from a lady who had been there that day. She had asked me to pray for her son, because the two of them were estranged. We prayed that the mind-blinding spirit that had caused this rift would be removed and that reconciliation would come. That very night, she received a very warm e-mail from her son. He told her that he loved her, and she was so happy that she had to share this good news. When these types of stories get out, this builds our authority because others recognize what we have known all along — that Christ is in us and that He is doing His work through us.

Our authority becomes effective only as we believe it, receive it, step into it and begin to act on it. We must know what the Word declares:

He who is in you is greater than he who is in the world.

1 John 4:4

UNDERSTANDING THE PRICE OF AUTHORITY

Most believers do not yet understand the authority that has been given to them in Christ, and therefore some misunderstand us when we act in authority. They say, "Who do they think they are? Boy, do they talk big." When you walk fully in the authority of the believer, you may pay a price.

This authority does not come to us because we sit in a class or attend a seminar. This comes through a day-in and a day-out walking with the Lord. Ask anyone who has such authority, and he or she will tell you that this is true. Authority comes at a price.

Many times we admire others and think to ourselves, *I like what that person has, and I want it*. But it's not that easy. There is a price to be paid.

When God called me into full-time ministry, I had been feeling for a very long while that this was what He wanted me to do. The truth is that I had known it since I was five, for at that early age, God began to speak to me. But, because of the circumstances of life, I had not been able to step into that calling until I was well into my adult life. I remember very vividly what happened when that day finally came.

I heard the Lord that day as clearly as I have ever heard any voice, although it did not come to me audibly, but in my spirit. He said, "Count the costs."

I had to think about that for a while, and I didn't respond immediately. I took time to speak with other people I trusted, and I took more time to pray. In the end, I decided that I would never be happy unless I did what I knew God wanted me to do. There is always a price to pay.

We cannot wave some ministry papers and expect Satan to obey us. We must spend time with God and with His Word.

Personally, I love to shop, and I would much rather be shopping than studying. But after I made a commitment to God and His ministry, I had to reset my priorities. There is a great responsibility contained in this call. I must put my flesh on notice of that fact. Sometimes I have to say to myself, "Sit down and be quiet; God's in charge, and you have made a commitment to Him. Now, do what He tells you to do."

The ministry of healing is a wonderful one, but if you want to be part of it, you must reorder your life. In the Healing Rooms, we need committed and serious people who are dedicated to the healing of those who are hurting. We need people who are walking with God and in His authority.

ALWAYS ACT WITH RESPECTABILITY AND HONOR

Whatever you do, act with respectability and honor, as representatives of the Lord Jesus Christ. Authority is never the same as physical power over someone, and it is never the power to lord it over others. It is always a spiritual force that God directs by His Word.

Jesus didn't go into a place like a bull in a china shop; He always went in with humility. And when we walk in humility, we can be as bold as we wish. Humility mixed with God's love paves the way for us to be greatly used by God and to stand in His authority and declare healing for many.

Now, let us examine our anointing to bring healing to the world today.

CHAPTER THREE

AN ANOINTING FOR THE HEALING MINISTRY TODAY

And it shall come to pass in that day, that his burden shall be taken away from off thy shoulder, and his yoke from off thy neck, and the yoke shall be destroyed BE-CAUSE OF THE ANOINTING.   Isaiah 10:27, KJV

It is nothing about us that brings healing to sick people. It is the anointing of God's Holy Spirit upon us. What is this anointing that we speak of so much? It is nothing less than His presence and power residing in us for the work of the ministry.

The Scriptures have much to say about the anointing and about those who are anointed. For instance, David sang:

Therefore I will give thanks to You,
O Lord, among the Gentiles,
And sing praises to Your name.

Great deliverance He gives to His king,
And shows mercy to HIS ANOINTED,
To David and his descendants forevermore.
                                        Psalm 18:49-50

God has promised us *"great deliverance,"* and to *"show mercy to His anointed."* Mercy here speaks of practical help.

The Children's Bread

When we are ministering to individuals in the Healing Rooms, we lay hands on them and pray, and then we expect them to be healed, because God has placed a special anointing upon our lives for healing. He has promised to show forth a special mercy, a special practical help, through us, His servants, His anointed ones.

Humanity Touched by Divinity

We are very human, and at the moment we lay hands on others, we may well have problems and trials of our own to face, but when we lay hands on them for healing, something exciting happens. In that moment, we are God's anointed ones for that purpose.

This is why spiritual gifts, like the word of knowledge and the word of wisdom, often come to us in these situations. God miraculously reveals to us things that we would not otherwise have known, so that His *"great deliverance"* can come and His *"mercy"* can be shown.

Amazingly, some people suddenly receive a word of knowledge; they suddenly know something they had no way of knowing before. Others can quickly discern the presence of evil spirits. This is an extremely useful gift when ministering to the sick. If there is a spirit present, we can know that this spirit needs to be cast out before we continue ministering healing. Deliverance from demons is an essential part of the healing ministry. This all comes with the anointing.

In another psalm, David rejoiced:

Now I know that the LORD saves HIS ANOINTED;
He will answer him from His holy heaven
With the saving strength of His right hand.

Psalm 20:6

God protects us, His anointed, and watches over us so that we can perform that which we are called by Him to do. When we are where He has called us to be, and we are doing what He has called us to do, there will be an awesome umbrella of His protection over us. As long as we stay within that framework, we have nothing to fear. If we get out from under that umbrella of God's protection, we risk opening ourselves up to attack.

When we are under the anointing, we need have no fear to deal with the evil spirits often encoutered in the healing ministry. The problems many people are facing sometimes seem totally natural, but as we wait on the Spirit, He will show us what is at the root of them, often something much more sinister.

I have never felt personally called to what many are calling "the deliverance ministry," which often deals exclusively with demon spirits and their manifestations, but if someone needs deliverance in order to be healed, I'm ready to work for deliverance. It is just a matter of speaking out what we know by the Spirit and letting Him do the rest.

My particular anointing has been in teaching and in bringing people to the knowledge of God's will for healing. This is a vital part of the healing ministry, for we are showing God's people what they can believe for in their own lives as God's anointed.

> *I have found My servant David;*
> *With My holy oil I have ANOINTED him,*
> *With whom My hand shall be established;*
> *Also My arm shall strengthen him.*   Psalm 89:20-21

God had designated David to do His work, and because of that His promises for David were great. God would anoint David, establish him and strengthen him. That's exactly what God will do for all those who allow themselves to be used by Him today. This is important, for it is the anointing, the presence and power of God, that destroys the yokes and lifts heavy burdens — not anything that we do ourselves.

SPECIAL ANOINTINGS FOR SPECIAL WORKS

All believers can carry a general anointing with them wherever they go, but there is also a special anointing for special tasks. This is why we, normal everyday people, can see such extraordinary things accomplished under the anointing.

Other people may look upon us as merely a "next-door neighbor," a "friend" or a an "acquaintance." They may see us digging around in the dirt in our yards, sweeping off our front porches or doing some other such menial task. To them, we're just another human being, pretty much like everyone else. But when we get under the anointing, everything changes.

Many find this difficult to understand. How can we be "normal" one minute and an anointed minister the next. But this is nothing difficult to understand. It happens because God is suddenly working through us — as human and as normal as we otherwise are.

When people see us jogging or sunbathing, they may never imagine that we are so different at other times. It's the anointing that makes this difference.

There is an individual anointing, and there is a corporate anointing, and we should have both. In the Healing Rooms, we want both of these anointings flowing together in unity.

In prayer, for instance, we begin in our corporate anointing, and we all call upon God. Then, someone may step into his or her individual anointing and begin to give forth a special word revealed to him or her about the situation at hand. Whatever the case, learn to flow in your anointing, because it is the anointing that sets us free.

The Kingly Office

The work of the ministry is part of the kingly office of Christ, and a calling to this office is accompanied by many gifts that enable us to perform it. The anointing brings with itself gifts and abilities that are beyond our natural talents.

Jesus was the Anointed One, the Christ, and when His anointing functions through us, men and women are seeing Jesus working through human beings. He told us that it would be so:

> *"Most assuredly, I say to you, he who believes in Me, the works that I do he will do also; and greater works than these he will do, because I go to My Father."*
>
> John 14:12

We can do these *"greater works"* only because the Lord is manifesting His power and presence through us.

The Pull of the Anointing

Most of us have favorite ministries or favorite ministers who particularly bless us. We love to be in one of the crusades of those ministers, and when those men or women are flowing in the anointing, we find something attracting or pulling us to them. We know that this is God's presence on them, and we love them for it.

We may not know these individuals personally at all, but we deeply admire them because of the way we see

57

Christ coming forth from their lives. We know that it's not something about them personally; it's Jesus in them.

I have often said about my husband Bud that I would have loved him even if I hadn't been married to him. This is because I am blessed and drawn by the anointing of God on his life. What shines through Bud is more than his personality; it is the very touch of God.

When we get under the anointing, we are often amazed by what flows through us. The anointing working through us brings healing and deliverance to the sick in such unusual ways. What a wonderful experience it is to have God working through you! And that's exactly what happens in the healing ministry.

JESUS WAS ANOINTED

Jesus, as a man, recognized the anointing of God upon His life. He said:

> *The Spirit of the LORD is upon Me,*
> *Because He has ANOINTED Me to preach the gospel to the poor;*
> *He has sent Me to heal the brokenhearted,*
> *To proclaim liberty to the captives*
> *And recovery of sight to the blind,*
> *To set at liberty those who are oppressed;*
> *To proclaim the acceptable year of the LORD.* Luke 4:18-19

The things that God did through Jesus under the anointing are some of the same things the anointing will do through us, for God has chosen to place His anointing upon average people today. We may be chatting with a person one moment about today's weather, a local sale or some other such mundane subject, and the very next moment the river of God's refreshing will be flowing through that person in the Spirit. That one is suddenly and inexplicably changed by the anointing that is upon him or her for a particular work. Jesus said, *"He has anointed ME,"* and you can make that same claim when His Spirit comes upon you.

Isaiah spoke of this anointing destroying yokes and lifting heavy burdens. A yoke could represent any type of bondage, and God wants to deliver us from every bondage. Healing is clearly included.

As a prelude to the truths revealed in the synagogue in Capernaum, Luke tells us:

> *Then Jesus returned in the power of the Spirit to Galilee, and news of Him went out throughout all the surrounding region.*   Luke 4:14

When the Holy Ghost anointing comes upon a person, there is a demonstration of power and authority that cannot be denied. It draws the attention of others. Mark recorded the same phenomenon:

> *It came to pass in those days that Jesus came from Nazareth of Galilee, and was baptized by John in the Jordan. And immediately, coming up from the water, He saw the heavens parting and the Spirit descending upon Him like a dove. Then a voice came from heaven, "You are My beloved Son, in whom I am well pleased."*
> Mark 1:9-11

From that day forward, Jesus was different, and when the anointing comes upon us, we will be different too.

It was the anointing upon the life of Jesus that enabled Him to *"do good"* and to *"heal all who were oppressed"*:

59

THE CHILDREN'S BREAD

... how God anointed Jesus of Nazareth with the Holy
Spirit and with power, who went about doing good and
healing all who were oppressed of the devil, for God
was with Him.   Acts 10:38

When the anointing came upon Jesus, He was unmis-
takably and radically changed, and we can also be changed
by the anointing today. Jesus was able to go about *"doing*
good," and we can too. He was able to bring healing to
"all who were oppressed of the devil," and we can too — under the anointing.

These are not things that we will do in our own
strength, but when the anointing is upon us, we cannot
not do them. It is the Lord working through us.

DID JESUS REALLY NEED THE ANOINTING?

Some might think that Jesus could have done anything
of Himself, but that was not so. He Himself said:

"Most assuredly, I say to you, the Son can do nothing
of Himself, but what He sees the father do; for what-
ever He does, the Son also does in like manner."
                                                  John 5:19

Unless He chose to work within the framework of submission to His heavenly Father and therefore receive His
anointing for the assigned work, He could not do that
work. And Jesus was an example for all of us. If you expect to have the anointing at work in your life, you must
place yourself in submission to the Father and receive His
anointing.

Jesus said this on more than one occasion:

An Anointing for the Healing Ministry Today

"When you lift up the Son of Man, then you will know that I am He, and that I do nothing of Myself; but as My Father taught Me, I speak these things." John 8:28

Our legal right to act, which carries with it an authority, a power, a *dunamis*, or dynamite from God, is based on our willingness to submit to Him in all things. If even Jesus needed the Creator's power, how much more do we need it today? Jesus said He could do *"nothing"* of Himself as a man. Think about that!

Jesus knew how to get the anointing flowing in His life and how to keep it flowing, and everything He did was setting an example for us. Jesus was an obedient servant, and we must learn to emulate His example.

Doing the Impossible Under the Anointing

God is urging us to call those things that be not as though they were. Paul wrote to the Romans:

... (as it is written, "I have made you the father of many nations") in the presence of Him whom he believed — God, who gives life to the dead and calls those things which do not exist as though they did. Romans 4:17

We can do this impossible task only under the unction of the Holy Ghost.

By faith we understand that the worlds were framed by the word of God, so that the things which are seen were not made of things which are visible. Hebrews 11:3

The very universe and all that is in it came about from nothing. God spoke it into existence. This is what is possible under the anointing of God. Sometimes as I ride down our highways and contemplate all that God has made on either side of me, I am amazed. How perfect it is! And God made it all just by speaking. What power! What authority! And it is all available to us through the anointing.

"POWER [THE ANOINTING] HAD GONE OUT OF HIM"

And Jesus, immediately knowing in Himself that power had gone out of Him, turned around in the crowd and said, "Who touched My clothes?"   Mark 5:30

What was it that Jesus felt that day? How did He know that someone had touched His clothes? He knew because when the anointing comes out of you, you feel it. When I minister to people and they receive, I sense it. It's almost like a little butterfly moving out of my hands, flowing out of me.

Some people just pull it out of you, but there are others you pray for, and you don't feel anything. Or you feel the anointing flowing from you and then bouncing back to you — because it has not been received.

THE ANOINTING IS TRANSFERABLE

The anointing is transferable. That's why we lay hands on the sick, and they recover. With the apostle Paul, other means were used to transfer the anointing:

Now God worked unusual miracles by the hands of Paul, so that even handkerchiefs or aprons were brought from his body to the sick, and the diseases left them and the evil spirits went out of them.   Acts 19:11-12

These were indeed *"unusual miracles."* According to some, the cloths that Paul used, which are here called *"aprons,"* were actually rags that were tied around his hips to absorb perspiration as he ministered. Such rags were used to send healing to the sick because there was a special anointing on them.

Nowadays, we use small pieces of cloth, and we lay our hands on them, anoint them with oil and pray over them so that they can be sent out to homes where sick and suffering people are. And God is still doing *"unusual miracles"* today.

Later, an even more unusual miracle began to happen with the disciples. As they were leaving certain towns, their shadows passed over some sick who had not yet been attended to, and those people were healed. This act did not seem to be deliberate or thoughtout by the disciples as were the miracles of the handkerchiefs and aprons. Without them even realizing it, God used their presence (or rather, His presence in them) to bring healing to the sick.

This is similar to the miracle of those who were healed just by touching the hem of Jesus' garment:

> *[They] begged Him that they might only touch the hem of His garment. And as many as touched it were made perfectly well.*   Matthew 14:36

Why was it that the people sought to touch the hem of His garment and not some other place? This was important to the release of their faith:

> *Again the LORD spoke to Moses, saying, "Speak to the children of Israel: Tell them to make tassels on the corners of their garments throughout their generations, and to put a blue thread in the tassels of the corners. And*

you shall have the tassel, that you may look upon it and remember all the commandments of the LORD and do them, and that you may not follow the harlotry to which your own heart and your own eyes are inclined, and that you may remember and do all My commandments, and be holy for your God. I am the LORD your God, who brought you out of the land of Egypt, to be your God: I am the LORD your God." Numbers 15:37-41

When the woman with the issue of blood said, "If I can only touch the hem of His garment," she was saying, "I must touch God's promise, for it is anointed and that anointing destroys every yoke and lifts every burden. If I can do that, I know I will be set free." She was able to touch it, and she was indeed made whole.

As I minister in the Healing Rooms and in the Bible school, I can see the anointing I have being transferred to others. Jesus said to His disciples:

"Heal the sick, cleanse the lepers, raise the dead, cast out demons. Freely you have received, freely give."
Matthew 10:8

Whatever we have is for the purpose of blessing others, and it can also be shared. It isn't ours; it was given by God for the benefit of the entire Body of Christ. Don't hold it back. Release it to others.

When we pray for people in the Healing Rooms, we believe for the anointing to come upon them too. We want to minister healing to them, but we also want to see them stand on their own and very possibly minister to others who need healing. They need our prayers now, but later, many others will need their prayers.

An Anointing for the Healing Ministry Today

The Anointing Is Available

The anointing, the electricity of God, can still accomplish these same works today, and we need it. But what good does it do to have a light switch if you never turn it on? What good does it do for you to have the anointing of God Almighty upon your life if you never put it to use?

The anointing is available. Get plugged in to it and put it to work in your life.

The Anointing Overcomes All Fear

Ministry is a fearful responsibility, and before I minister I always ask the Lord to let me know that He is with me. Days and weeks before the event, I feel ready to go and excited about the prospect. But when it comes right down to it, I begin to feel the fearsome responsibility of what I am about to do, and I begin to wonder: *What am I doing? And why am I doing this? I shouldn't be here? I don't think I even can do this.*

Suddenly, I want to run away. "Let me out of the car," I want to say. I'm not sure I understand fully this reaction because I know that I'm called to do it, and I really want to do it. I guess this is just a very human reaction.

When I get ready to do the thing God has called me to do, I see my own fleshly limitations, and it frightens me. *What in the world was I thinking?* I wonder. Once I am standing in front of the people, however, it is an entirely different feeling. I suddenly feel so much power that I think I can do anything.

Part of this may be the result of the Word I am preaching building my own faith, but surely this phenomenon can only be explained by the anointing that

65

comes upon us to do the Lord's work. The anointing changes everything.

THE ANOINTING IS ACTIVATED BY FAITH

It also works the other way around. Faith activates the anointing within us, and draws it out. When we lay hands on sick people, and we know that God will work, something always happens. All we have to do is be obedient — whether we feel anything or not.

When the woman of Mark 5:27-28 heard about Jesus, her faith was activated. Hearing about Jesus, she pressed her way through the crowd and touched His garment. She knew that if she would do that, she would be made whole.

When Romans 2:17 says, *"Faith cometh by hearing, and hearing by the word of God"* (KJV), it doesn't mean just hearing one time. Once we have heard it, we need to hear it again and again. When I teach, I repeat certain important principles often, and each time I repeat them, I feel the power of them. What precious promises! The anointing activated by our faith brings results.

THE ANOINTING BRINGS PROTECTION

In ancient times, when anointing oil was rubbed on the sheep, it served many purposes. For one, it kept bugs from attacking and bothering them. Since the anointing is the power and presence of Almighty God, nothing could be more protective. Things that have tormented us before will suddenly keep their distance from us.

When the anointing comes, the presence and character of God comes with it, and demons are uncomfortable around Him.

THE ANOINTING REQUIRES PREPARATION

We must prepare for the anointing, and that requires paying a certain price. Jesus said, *"The Spirit of the Lord is upon me,"* and then He went on to enumerate the things God had called Him to do under the anointing. But He had to go through a period of preparation, a wilderness experience, and we are often required to endure such testings before we are ready to step out in healing ministry.

When God rubs the anointing into us, He is placing His own character within us. Some of us need a second rub. And more than that: We need to listen, study, fellowship and seek, for this is all part of building the needed anointing.

The Old Testament was a shadow of good things to come, and the New Testament represents the substance of those things. That means that you and I have the real thing. His name is Jesus. He is our substance, and we know it. We feel His presence and His power. Get ready to do His work.

THE ANOINTING IS CONTAGIOUS

Elisha recognized that association with powerful and important people was important. He said to Elijah, his mentor:

> *"As the LORD lives, and as your soul lives, I will not leave you!"*   2 Kings 2:2 and 4

Just as running with the wrong crowd will rub off on us spiritually, association with those who have the anointing will bring about the power of Almighty God in our lives. Elisha knew that Elijah's anointing would rub off on him — if he just stayed close to the prophet. This is a lesson to all of us. Stay close to the anointing, and spend the necessary time in preparation for the ministry God has for you.

Elijah went to Gilgal, and Elisha followed him. The purpose for their going there was to be anointed, and there faith began to move. It was in Gilgal that they began to live by faith.

Then Elijah moved on to Bethel, and you and I also must move on to that place. Bethel is the place of decisions, and at Bethel the decision will be made as to whether or not we move forward or backward. I would advise you to never go backward and to always move forward.

It is at Bethel that the decision will be made about winning or losing. Will we go on with God? Or will we turn back? As with Jacob, there may be some wrestling taking place at Bethel. As Gilgal represents faith, Bethel represents death to self. There we make the fateful decision.

Next, Elijah and Elisha were off to Jericho, and Jericho was a place of warfare. It was in Jericho that Joshua and the children of Israel had been tested in battle before they were allowed to proceed into the Promised Land. At Jericho, all fear of the enemy must die. There every knee must bow, and there every battle is won. We win, the devil loses and the anointing flows.

At Jericho, great steps of faith were taken. Joshua told the people to march around the walls of that fortified city for seven days. On the seventh day, those stout walls came down — because of the anointing, because God's people had come by faith.

Next, Elijah went on to Jordan. Even after our walls come down, we must move on and continue progressing. Elisha refused to leave Elijah.

Jordan is the place where we get a clear vision. When Elisha saw Elijah going up, he saw the glory of God, the mantle, upon him and knew that he wanted it. "That's mine," he said. "That's what I've been waiting for. That's what I came here for." He reached out for it, and, with it, he received a double portion.

If you and I really desire this anointing for the ministry of healing, we must make a quality decision to seek until we find it. And one sure way to receive it is to stay close to those who have it demonstrated in their lives.

When you make such a decision, you will go through some tough times, and you will pass through some times of confusion concerning just what your future holds. Eventually, however, as you persevere, your vision will become clear, and you will know exactly what God wants you to do.

When you have received a clear vision that leads to a powerful anointing, no man and no demon spirit will be allowed to get in your way.

When you see someone who has a gift that you know God is calling you to, fellowship with that person. Rub shoulders with that person, because the anointing will come off on to you by association.

Before you rush into something, count the cost. Don't answer too quickly, because you don't want to have to back down later. Consider it carefully. Know that you are willing to pay the price. From the day you accept His call, God will expect more of you than is expected of others; this is because you have agreed to take on His presence in a fuller degree.

There are things that we can do to invite the anointing, and there are also some things we should avoid because they detract from the anointing. Here are some of them.

AVOID CRITICIZING THE ANOINTING

We cannot see the Holy Spirit, and we cannot see the anointing, but we surely can see the actions the anointing produces. If you're in the Spirit as you minister to sick people, you will often sense that the Spirit is "all over them." Sometimes they are visibly affected by it. Some turn crimson; others tremble; and still others begin to bat their eyes or in some other way let you know that they are feeling God's power.

Years ago, when I first witnessed people shaking under the anointing, I was offended by it and wondered why people thought they had to do that. *That's not necessary,* I was thinking. *In fact, it's ridiculous.* But before long, it began to happen to me too. I had to repent of my bad attitude and ask God to forgive me. We have no right to be critical of how others react to the anointing because we don't know how we might react in the same situation.

The Spirit is like the wind. We can't see the wind, but we sure can see the effects of it. Jesus said:

> *"The wind blows where it wishes, and you hear the sound of it, but cannot tell where it comes from or where it goes. So is everyone who is born of the Spirit."*
>
> John 3:8

What a beautiful truth! We can easily see the effects of the anointing. As the Spirit moves, God's presence and power are manifested.

When Jesus was speaking with Mary and Martha about their brother who had died and been already in the grave for three days, He asked a question:

> *"Did I not say to you that if you would believe you would see the glory of God?"*
> John 11:40

When the glory of God comes, there is something to "*see.*" His presence produces something, something visible, something noticeable. When the glory of God comes upon us, it produces many varied reactions. Some want to get down and roll on the floor. Others want to run and shout and jump. Others want to sing and dance. And still others cry. Let God be God, and don't try to limit or control these responses to His Spirit.

One of the most wonderful manifestations of God's presence is His love. It warms us, and suddenly we love those whom we haven't cared for in the past. We *really* love them. God is love, and when He is in us, we can love too. Just as He loves everyone, we can love everyone. This is an important element in the healing ministry.

Sometimes the anointing comes in fire; sometimes it come as a cloud; sometimes it comes as a dove; sometimes it comes as oil; sometimes it comes as water; and sometimes it comes as wind. These are all symbols of the Holy Spirit spoken of in the Scriptures, and God is free to manifest them as He wills to reveal His presence.

Recently, Bud and I visited a nearby Bible camp, and during the prayer at the end of one of the meetings in the sanctuary, I suddenly smelled something burning and saw fingers of smoke rising upward. I started to turn to Bud to ask what was happening when I suddenly realized that my eyes had not been open. I had closed them for the prayer, and what I was seeing and smelling was in the spirit, not in the flesh.

I told Bud what I had experienced and we prayed about what it could mean. The next morning we were having breakfast with another man and his wife, and I told them about the experience and asked what they thought it could mean. "Well," the man answered, "I suppose the first question is: What did it smell like?"

I found it to be a very interesting question. The truth was that I hadn't really thought about it. Now that I did, I realized that it had actually had a very peculiar smell, like burning flesh. The thing was that I had never before smelled burning flesh. This, however, seemed to be the only way I could describe what I had smelled. "Let's just pray about that," the man said.

Over time, I came to the conclusion that this experience meant that God, in His mercy, was consuming more of my flesh and that what I had seen was the altar of incense. I had been praying that He would open the eyes of my understanding, that I would see more deeply into the spirit realm, that I would receive new strategies and ideas from the Lord, that I would begin to see things through His eyes, and that I would see more clearly the enemy and his tactics. What I was really praying for, I suppose, was a discerning of the spirits, for I was asking to look into the spirit realm.

Over the next five weeks I had many dreams and visions, and God showed me many peculiar things as a result of that prayer. And when that period of searching had ended, I was seeing more clearly into the spirit realm than ever before. I was seeing things I had never seen before and hearing things I had never heard before.

We need spiritual eyes to see what the enemy is doing and also to see things the way God sees them. As He opens the eyes of our understanding, then we flow in a greater anointing.

The interesting thing about my prayer and its results is that I had never before had a desire to pray such a prayer. I had heard it taught, but that teaching hadn't captured my attention. Suddenly, it grabbed me, I prayed it and the result was wonderful.

God's desire is to move us from victory to victory and from glory to glory, so that there is a constant growth in our lives. We can grow in the anointing.

Avoid Common Sins That Can Hinder Your Anointing

There are many common sins that will hinder your anointing for healing, so you want to avoid them at all costs. The first thing that can hinder your anointing is unbelief. It even hindered Jesus:

> *Now He did not do many mighty works there because of their unbelief.*   Matthew 13:58

> *Now He could no mighty work there, except that He laid His hands on a few sick people and healed them. And He marveled because of their unbelief. Then He went about the villages in a circuit, teaching.*   Mark 6:5-6

Imagine! Jesus *"could do no mighty work there,"* and He attributed it to *"their unbelief."* Unbelief, then, can prevent the anointing from flowing.

There can be no doubt that Jesus was anointed, and that He was anointed always. He was not just having a bad day on this occasion. Still, as strong as Jesus was in the Spirit, He could not function under the anointing on that occasion because the spirit of unbelief was so strong in that place. As a result, He looked for other places to minister.

But what did Jesus do in those other places when He found them? He went from place to place *"teaching."* He recognized that He needed to bring the people into a higher level of faith so that they could believe for His miracles and so that He could minister to them.

Strive to remain free from this insidious sin of unbelief, and when you find yourself hindered by it, move on to other places where you can teach people faith.

Another thing that can adversely affect your anointing is unforgiveness:

> *Then Peter came to Him and said, "Lord, how often shall my brother sin against me, and I forgive him? Up to seven times?"*
> *Jesus said to him, "I do not say to you, up to seven times, but up to seventy times seven."*   Matthew 18:21-22

Don't be foolish enough to allow a root of bitterness to take hold within your spirit. Deal with unforgiveness quickly and decisively and remain free of it.

Matthew recorded these words of Jesus:

> *"Assuredly, I say to you, whatever you bind on earth will be bound in heaven, and whatever you loose on earth will be loosed in heaven.*
> *"Again I say to you that if two of you agree on earth concerning anything that they ask, it will be done for them by My Father in heaven."*   Matthew 18:18-19

Sometimes, in order to be free in the anointing, we need to do some loosing and some binding, and sometimes we need to agree together — that is to stand together in authority. These acts will often free the anointing to flow in us. When your power seems to be bound, take some or all of these actions.

The anointing flows more readily when we combine forces. That's why Jesus went on to say:

> *"For where two or three are gathered together in My name, I am there in the midst of them."*
>
> Matthew 18:20

There can be no question but that agreement among brothers frees the anointing to flow.

Others sins that can hinder your anointing are stubbornness and rebellion. Samuel reprimanded King Saul for these very sins:

> *"Has the LORD as great delight in burnt offerings and sacrifices,*
> *As in obeying the voice of the LORD?*
> *Behold, to obey is better than sacrifice,*
> *And to heed than the fat of rams.*
> *For rebellion is as the sin of witchcraft,*
> *And stubbornness is as iniquity and idolatry.*
>
> 1 Samuel 15:22-23

King Saul lost his throne because he was not willing to let go of his own desires and obey God. This stubbornness cost him everything and led to outright rebellion. Stubborn and rebellious people cut themselves off from God's anointing, because He is not about to share His soverignty with anyone else.

Another of the plagues of our modern day that robs many of their anointing is yielding to sinful pleasures. If there is sin in your life, deal with it quickly, through Jesus:

> *If we confess ours sins, He is faithful and just to forgive us our sins and to cleanse us from all unrighteousness.*
>
> 1 John 1:9

Get rid of anything unclean in your life because it will surely hinder your anointing, and you cannot afford to allow that to happen.

I have also found that sadness, or brokenheartedness, can adversely affect the anointing. Jesus was called to *"heal the brokenhearted"* and to set the captives free. Let Him heal your broken heart and set you free:

THE CHILDREN'S BREAD

The Spirit of the LORD is upon Me, ...
He has sent Me to heal the brokenhearted. Luke 4:18

Those who have been hurt and who feel despondent and downtrodden need God's touch today. Let the Spirit move on you so that you can have an anointing to minister to others. Feel the love of God being poured into you, and then turn around and pour it back into others.

Another thing that will hinder your anointing is a lack of total submission to the Lord. Because Jesus was God, He had the anointing without measure (see John 3:34). You and I are much more limited. We know that with God all things are possible, but we also know that we are much more limited as men and women. This is why we so desperately need the anointing. When the little bit of wisdom and power we have is expended, we must rely upon Him who has no limitations.

For this reason, total submission to the Lord is necessary in this ministry of healing. We cannot be telling God what to do. Instead, we listen for Him to direct us. We seek His face, asking Him to do the work through us. Then we know that the work will be done, for it is Him doing it.

Another thing that hinders the anointing is confusion about what we are asking God to do. Jesus had a habit of asking people what they wanted before He ministered to them. That way they couldn't change their minds in midstream, and there was no confusion about what was being sought. This freed His anointing to work.

If the devil can prevent us from believing that we are healed, he can keep us bound. His tactic is to keep us in confusion and pain. He delights in making a mess of your life. And sickness is just part of his arsenal. He will use anything at all, anything, to try to destroy you.

The enemy will try to cause your car to break down. He

will try to cause problems for you with the people with whom you work. He will make every effort to keep your life filled with as much confusion as possible because he wants to put out your fire. You must learn how to drive a stake and declare, "This far and no farther, Satan."

On the famous *Ed Sullivan Show*, Ed always had some jugglers. They would come out juggling plates in the air. Then they would run back and get something else and put it into the mix until it seemed impossible for them to keep everything in the air at the same time.

This is what the devil will do to us if we let him, and soon something will come crashing down. We have the authority not to allow him to do this.

For those who fail to be obedient to the Lord, the anointing becomes a very heavy load indeed. It may stay with them for a time, but if they persist in their ways, it will eventually leave them entirely.

AVOID GETTING OUTSIDE YOUR ANOINTING

Each office — that of apostle, prophet, evangelist, pastor or teacher — has its own anointing. The anointing goes with the office, and if we persevere in the office to which we are called, then we have a right to claim the anointing that goes with that office.

There are also particular ministries that the Lord gives to each of us, and there is likewise a special anointing that goes with each of these particular ministries. At one point, the Lord told me to stop preaching and teaching other things and to stay within the special realm of faith and healing He had assigned to me. As I have done that, I have been blessed with a greater anointing.

Not long after the Lord told me that, another subject was assigned to me to teach in the Bible school, and I taught it,

77

but I sensed that the anointing was not as great upon it, and the fruit was less visible as a result. I was happy when that particular semester ended.

Then, again, I was asked to teach a different subject. I hated to refuse, so I tried to prepare for that subject, and I found that I couldn't do it. Several weeks before the classes were to begin, I still had very little prepared to give. *What will I do?* I wondered.

I also began having some headaches during that time, and I was asking God why. One day I attended a special meeting where I heard a minister say: "Many times, when we have a manifestation in our bodies, if we can get alone with God and ask, 'Why am I having this manifestation?' He'll show us the root of it."

He asked us all to find a place of prayer and to ask the Lord what was causing the thing we were experiencing. I did that, and before long, the Lord said to me, "I told you I didn't want you teaching anything but healing and faith. This is your own fault."

As soon as I got home, I told Bud what I was feeling. "I can't teach that other subject," I told him.

"It's too late to change your mind now," he said. "There are only a few weeks before class begins. How could they replace you at this late date?"

"I don't know," I said, "but I know I can't do it."

"You have to do it," he said.

"But I'm not," I countered. "God told me not to do it."

"Then I'll have to teach it myself," he offered.

"Well, you may have to," I agreed.

But when I called the office and told one of my supervisors what I was feeling, it turned out that someone else had been wanting to teach that particular class. That person was very grateful to me for being willing to give up the class, but I was just being obedient to God. When we get out of our anointing, we are not protected.

Things That Can Build Your Anointing

There are some simple things that we can do to build our anointing. The anointing comes, for instance, as we spend more time with God. We become like those with whom we fellowship. It is true in the natural, and it is also true in the spiritual. As parents, we are sometimes not very happy about our children's choice of friends. We don't like those people, and we're afraid that their bad habits will rub off on our children. And it is a very real danger.

Who we fellowship with is important. If you and I have enough fellowship with the Holy Ghost, His nature and His ways will rub off on us, and we will thus develop an anointing.

For another thing, I love to spend time in the promises of the Word of God. This is because they are so anointed. In this way, I derive much of my anointing from the Word of God. Because of this, I am personally convinced that those who minister healing must keep themselves in the Word to maintain their anointings.

Being immersed in the Word of God keeps us sharpened to the possibilities in Him and prevents us from becoming stale. In His Word, we continually discover new and more wonderful promises, and this keeps us moving forward in the Spirit.

A Great Future in the Anointing

God has many things He can entrust to us in the future, as He sees that we are obedient to Him and walk in His power and authority. Or He can withdraw His call to us any time we begin to think that the power and authority are ours. We are not our own masters. Even Jesus had to submit to the Father in all things, and the choice is ours.

It is always very exciting to begin to see the anointing of the Spirit flow in your life. You suddenly begin to say things and do things that you have never said or done before. You wonder what possessed you to put a time on a promise you give someone in the Spirit. You know in yourself that you are incapable of placing such dates on things, yet you have done it. Your mind tells you that you should not have said it, but it spontaneously came forth, without your having thought about it. Now, it's up to the Lord to fulfill it. This is the flow of the anointing, and we can look forward to greater and greater things in the future as we stay in the anointing.

Now, let's examine practical ways that you can receive healing for yourself and how you can minister it to others.

CHAPTER FOUR

HOW TO BRING HEALING TO YOURSELF AND TO OTHERS

There are several key things we need to do to get ourselves and others healed. In this chapter, I wish to outline some of these important keys.

HAVE FAITH AND HELP OTHERS TO HAVE FAITH

So then faith comes by hearing, and hearing by the word of God.   Romans 10:17

First, we must somehow produce faith — in ourselves (when we need healing) or in the people to whom we are ministering healing. Without faith, none of us can receive anything from the Lord. Faith is His simple requirement to possess His promises. He is a faith God, and whatever we receive from Him, we must receive by faith. Afterward, we must learn how to release our faith — in ourselves and in the people to whom we minister — but first it must be produced.

How can we produce faith in those who need healing? This may sound extremely difficult to some, but in reality, it's very simple. Since faith comes by hearing the Word of God, we can produce faith in others by giving them that Word, by affirming to them what God has promised to do for them. Men and women don't get healed by having faith in what men have to say (and if they can't get their minds off of what men say and onto what God says, they often won't be healed at all).

Men's words are often filled with doubt, with fear and with discouragement. Sometimes men *do* agree with what God says, and if they are quoting Him or if what they say agrees with what God says, we can know that their messages are from God. But too often what men say is the exact opposite of what God says, and because of that, their words actually work against our healing.

Philosophy cannot bring healing. A good sermon cannot bring healing. It is the power of the Word of God — when it is believed and obeyed — that produces miracles of healing in our bodies. There is a healing anointing upon the promises of the Scriptures.

We have many examples of healing in the biblical records of Jesus' ministry. Of the nineteen individual cases mentioned in the four gospels, we can see clearly the strong role faith played in at least a dozen of those cases. Faith in God is what produces healing. When men and women believe, they receive. So we must strengthen their faith any way we can.

Every act we perform in the healing ministry must be performed by faith, and it must be received by faith. The laying on of hands should always produce healing, because Jesus said: *"They will lay hands on the sick, and they will recover"* (Mark 16:18). But if hands are laid on people, and they do not believe, they will not be healed.

Faith is not just saying, "I believe." Sometimes we say it, and the truth of it has not yet reached our spirits. Rehearsing God's promises can stir faith in us or in those to whom we minister. Hide those promises in your heart, and when you need to use them, either for yourself or for others, the Spirit will quicken them to you. If you believe, your faith will move others to believe also.

The Nobleman Who Believed:

Jesus told of a nobleman to whom He spoke, and the man believed. It's a wonderful story:

> So Jesus came again to Cana of Galilee where He had made the water wine. And there was a certain nobleman whose son was sick at Capernaum. When he heard that Jesus had come out of Judea into Galilee, he went to Him and implored Him to come down and heal his son, for he was at the point of death. Then Jesus said to him, "Unless you people see signs and wonders, you will by no means believe."
> The nobleman said to Him, "Sir, come down before my child dies!"   John 4:46-49

We can understand where this man was coming from because we've all been in this same position at one time or another, so desperate that we didn't want to hear more talk. "Just do something," we pled.

Jesus was ready to comply, and the man was ready to believe, so the miracle happened:

> Jesus said to him, "Go your way; your son lives." So the man believed the word that Jesus spoke to him, and he went his way.   John 4:50

When God says it, and we believe it, it happens. It's just that simple. Nothing else is needed.

This nobleman had not yet seen anything at all. He was away from home and could not know what was happening back there at this moment — or if anything at all was

83

happening. Yet, he believed. Faith does not depend on the presence of outward manifestations; faith believes without seeing.

Sometimes God sends physical manifestations to accompany a prayer or some other form of healing ministry, and sometimes He doesn't. Our faith must not be in the manifestation, but in what God has said. The man believed and went his way.

I like that. "Okay," he was saying to Jesus. "You said it; I believe it; and that settles it. My son is healed." And, of course, his faith produced the desired result:

> *And as he was now going down, his servants met him and told him, saying, "Your son lives!"*
> *Then he inquired of them the hour when he got better. And they said to him, "Yesterday at the seventh hour the fever left him." So the father knew that it was at the same hour in which Jesus said to him, "Your son lives." And he himself believed, and his whole household.*
> *This again is the second sign Jesus did when He had come out of Judea into Galilee.* John 4:51-54

This is an anointed example from the Scriptures of what we each need to do. If you need healing, this is the way you will receive it; and if you need to minister healing to others, this is the way you will do it. Stir faith in men's hearts.

SPEAK FAITH:

Speak faith to sick people, for that's what they need. If you are impressed by how terrible a person's sickness is, how will that person have faith for healing? If you are overcome by the difficulty of a particular case, who will help that person? If what a person has frightens you, how will that person ever believe for deliverance? Someone has to know what God says, and someone has to be willing to speak it forth. Be that person, and you will see results.

Sick people need their faith built up — even if they are very good Christians — because sickness has a way of dragging us down. Aches and pains work on our spirits, and have a depressing effect on us. Sick people often have trouble praying for themselves, because they know what they are feeling and what they are experiencing. This works against their faith in the Scriptures. Someone needs to stand firmly beside these individuals and declare what God says about the situation.

Many of us wait until we are sick to start learning the healing promises, but that's not the time. When your head is swimming, your stomach is churning and your back is aching, it's hard for you to have a clear mind to consider the promises of the Scriptures. The doctrine of divine healing does not mean that we will never get sick, so we must prepare for that eventuality. Divine healing means that when we do get sick, we will get well again — because we know and claim God's promises.

We live in a broken world, and bad things will happen to us from time to time. There are also other reasons for our being sick. There are sins that we often do not consider, the sins of omission.

Exercise Personal Faith:

There is a very personal element to faith that each of us needs. Sometimes we believe that God can do miracles, but we don't believe He will do them for us today. We need to believe not only that God heals, but that God wants to heal *us*. Most people believe that it's God's will to heal — in a general sense. They're just not sure that God wants to heal *them* and that He wants to do it *today*.

But God has declared that He is not a *"respecter of persons"* (KJV); in other words, He *"shows no partiality"*:

> Then Peter opened his mouth and said: "In truth I perceive that God shows no partiality."   Acts 10:34

If God will heal someone else, then He will heal you too. Believe it, and don't let the enemy tell you anything different.

The enemy will try to tell you that God has healed a certain person "because he was such a good guy," and you can't expect Him to do that same thing for you because you are not nearly as perfect. What a terrible lie from Hell! Jesus took your sin in His own body on the tree, so you are just as good as the next person in this regard.

We are not healed because we are good; we are healed because Jesus is good. Just as we are not saved from sin because of our own merit, we are likewise not delivered from sickness because we deserve it. This is another of the free gifts of our God.

I may not merit healing, but the One who loved me and gave Himself for me has offered it to me anyway. The work has already been done at Calvary, and the only thing you and I need to do is believe it and receive it.

FAITH IN A FINISHED WORK:

After Jesus had hung on the cross for a while, He cried out, *"It is finished"* (John 19:30), and it was. He had done everything that needed to be done for our salvation, and He had done everything that needed to be done for our healing. He had finished the work the Father had sent Him to do — all of it — and He was ready to go home and resume His rightful place at the Father's right hand.

It is finished. There is nothing more to wait for. Know

and cause others to know that healing is for now. Paul confidently wrote:

> *There is therefore now no condemnation to those who are in Christ Jesus, who do not walk according to the flesh, but according to the Spirit.*　　Romans 8:1

By this, Paul didn't mean that everyone was already perfect, but rather that perfection was now available to us. In the same way, Paul could have said, "There is therefore now no sickness in those who are in Christ Jesus." The price has been paid (regardless of the fact that many Christians are still sick), and healing — complete healing — is available to us. Receive it and minister it freely to others.

Perfection Not Required

God doesn't expect us to be perfect before we can receive His blessings. When that word *perfect* is used in the Scriptures, it means "mature," not what we commonly mean by perfection. We all make mistakes, but when we do, we have an Advocate with the Father. It is easy to receive God's forgiveness. Get on your knees and repent of your wrongdoing, and He will do the rest. Pray, "Lord, help me; I don't want to keep doing this. I know it's not right." And He will hear that cry.

Paul knew, perhaps better than anyone, that we are not perfect. Still, he declared to the church at Roman:

> *Yet in all these things we are more than conquerors through Him who loved us.*　　Romans 8:37

"More than conquerors"! How wonderful! But what precisely does that mean? A conqueror is a person who goes out and fights a battle and wins, bringing home the spoils.

So, how can anyone be *"more than"* a conqueror? It means that somebody else has gone out and fought the battle, winning and bringing the spoils home to us. Jesus has given it all to us — eternal life and untold blessings along with it. That's how we are *"more than conquerors."*

So we can stop feeling sorry for ourselves, and we can start acting like the King's kids, because that's exactly what we are. If we can get that fact into our heads, it will change everything for us.

The secret, of course, is being *"in Christ Jesus."* Too many are still in the flesh, in the world. Get in Him, get in the Spirit, and you will quickly see that healing is for all of God's people today.

Stop listening to what others say about your health. Get into God and into His Word and become an example to the world of God's perfect will. When you do this, others will flock to you to know about the things Christ does which no man can do.

I'm not just interested in facts and figures. It's not about tapes and books. I want to see believers raised up, and I want the lost to be evangelized. I want to see men and women sitting under the teaching of the Word of God until they have an anointing for deliverance and healing that can change the world around them.

GETTING PEOPLE FREED UP TO RECEIVE:

We need to get people freed up to receive. What do I mean by that? I mean that you need to teach them so that they lose all their fears and hang-ups and can open up to God and take what He is offering. When Jesus was on the earth, there was no doubt that He could do anything. There was no demon too powerful for Him to cast out and no sickness too difficult for Him to cure. Still, the Bible states that in certain places, as we have seen, He could heal only very few. Why was that? Again, it was *"because of their un-belief"* (Matthew 13:58). And what did Jesus do in these situations? Was He discouraged? Did He give up on the people? No, He kept going to them and teaching them until faith began to come and they could receive.

WHERE FAITH BEGINS:

F.F. Bosworth has said that faith can come only when the will of God is known, and since we only have faith in what we know, it is time to get to know what the Word of God says about healing. If we want to minister healing, we simply must know what God's Word says about it.

We must teach people how to receive by faith, not to wait until they see some result. There are those who cannot believe until they see, but faith is not for what we can see. It is for what we cannot see. Anyone can believe if he sees. If we already see, we have no more need of faith. We need faith only for what is not yet seen.

Do whatever is necessary to stir faith in the hearts of those who need His healing touch. Mental assent is not enough. Memorizing a verse is not enough. Quoting the Scriptures is not enough. You must meditate on God's promises until they become truth for you, and you must encourage others to do the same.

Many of us read things in the Bible again and again. Then, one day, perhaps when we are going through some of life's trials, we suddenly read a passage again, and it suddenly takes on new meaning. We never saw it in this way before. Now we know what God wants to do, and we can believe for it to be done.

When those moments come, Satan has to step back, for you have turned into a veritable tiger of faith. You know what you have, and you won't be denied. Now, when you pray, things begin to happen. You have all your guns loaded and at the ready, and you suddenly know how to use them.

When this happens, suddenly your faith is moving mountains, and you have become a real threat to the enemy. You know the will of God, and the devil knows that you know it. You will be different from this day forward.

This is not to say that you will never feel fear. It is not to say that you will not face things that will cause you to tremble. It is to say that you will always respond: *"Greater is He who is in me than he who is in the world."* This will alert the enemy to the fact that you are now walking in truth, that there is no doubt in your mind and that if anyone has to move aside it won't be you. He'll have to move.

Far too many of us fear what the enemy can to do us. *What if he just mows us down?* Well, suppose he does. The very worst he can do to us is send us into the presence of God, where we'll be better off anyway. So, his worst would be the very best for us.

Refuse to fear the enemy. Refuse to run from him. Know your rights in God. Know what He has called you to do, and do it to the best of your ability until He takes you home.

And don't be afraid of making a mistake. We all make them, myself included. When I err, the blood of Jesus covers my error. And as I continue to stay before the Lord and to submit to His authority over my life, He watches over me and my errors become fewer. This doesn't mean that we will be perfect — not just yet.

GOD IS NO RESPECTER OF PERSONS:

We must understand and teach not only that God can heal us, but that He will. He is not a respecter of persons. This is where the Word of God becomes so important. When the devil comes to you (and, believe me, he will), you can stand strong. You will say one thing, and he will say just the opposite. If you didn't know the will of God in that moment, Satan could stump you. That would give him authority in that area of your life. So, the more of the Word of God you have in you, the more you will be able to raise a standard against him.

When anyone asks us, "Will the Lord do it?" our immediate reply should be positive: "Yes, He will." This is God's desire, and it is made very clear to us in the Scriptures. Get that fact firmly rooted in your heart.

The promises of God are very exciting because they are so affirming, so positive, so steadfast and unchanging. Sometimes we can feel absolutely lousy, but when we begin to read the Bible or we put on a tape of someone ministering the Word — especially when it is done with authority and anointing — the Spirit comes and touches us, and we are made whole. Build faith for healing.

How Miracles Happen:

One day I asked God to show me how miracles happen. I was believing Him to use me in miracles, and so I wanted to understand them better. I knew that miracles were gifts from God and that they came by faith, but I wanted to know much more. The Lord led me to Luke 1:28.

> *And having come in, the angel said to her, "Rejoice, highly favored one, the Lord is with you; blessed are you among women!"* Luke 1:28

What a shocking experience that must have been! What was Mary's reaction to this strange appearance? And what happened next?

> *But when she saw him, she was troubled at his saying, and considered what manner of greeting this was. Then the angel said to her, "Do not be afraid, Mary, for*

*you have found favor with God. And behold, you will
conceive in your womb and bring forth a Son, and shall
call His name JESUS. He will be great, and will be called
the Son of the Highest: and the Lord God will give Him
the throne of His father David. And He will reign over
the house of Jacob forever, and of His kingdom there will
be no end."*

*Then Mary said to the angel, "How can this be, since I
do not know a man?"*

*And the angel answered and said to her, "The Holy Spirit
will come upon you, and the power of the Highest will
overshadow you; therefore, also, that Holy One who is
to be born will be called the Son of God."* Luke 1:29-35

Mary was understandably amazed by the announce-
ment of the angel that she would have a child. The reason
was that although she was *"betrothed"* to Joseph, they were
not yet married. Then God told her how the miracle would
happen. The Holy Spirit would come upon her and the
power of the Most High would overshadow her, and she
would receive something good and wonderful from the
Lord. That's how it happens.

The angel went on to give Mary some confirmation, telling her something that would strengthen her faith:

*"Now indeed, Elizabeth your relative has also conceived
a son in her old age; and this is now the sixth month for
her who was called barren. For with God nothing will
be impossible."* Luke 1:36-37

This is just what Mary needed to hear. What the angel
had told her seemed impossible, but God was also doing
the impossible in Elizabeth, and with Him, nothing is impossible. We have lots of impossibilities, but God has none.

This thing being done in Mary was in the hands of God, so it could not be impossible. When He is working, all things are possible.

Mary's response was the correct one:

> *Then Mary said, "Behold, the maidservant of the Lord! Let it be to me according to your word."*   Luke 1:38

Mary was willing to submit herself to God and to His special word for her life, and that must be our attitude as well. When a word comes from Him, however impossible it may seem, we can stand on it and allow it to jump-start our faith.

The Importance of a Rhema Word:

Such a personal word is wonderful. We have come to call it a *rhema* word from God, something He specifically speaks to our hearts. I have had this experience many times. I may be reading the Bible and reviewing all of its promises, and yet nothing seems to be happening. But then I seek God for some specific word for my life, a *rhema* word that I can cling to. When it comes, and it usually comes within twenty-four hours of the time I seek it, it gives me the faith I need for my miracle.

Many times such a word will come to me in the middle of the night. I am awakened, and that word just pops into my spirit. Sometimes it comes as I am getting out of bed to face another day. At other times, it comes to me as I am reading a portion of the Bible. However and whenever it comes, it is powerful and brings the desired result.

I would warn readers not to seek some special word from God unless and until you have made an effort to fill your heart with the *logos* Word, the written Word of God, found in the Bible.

The Children's Bread

Sometimes we hear someone else say something, and suddenly it becomes our own. Satan will always tell us that we are only thinking those thoughts because someone else has spoken them, but we know differently. Not everything that others say sparks something in our hearts. When it does, we can know that it was especially for us.

Understand and Help Others to Understand That Healing Is a Process

Most people receive healing through one of many processes. For example, we sometimes stand in a healing line in order to be ministered to by others. When our turn comes, we may feel tingly all over, or we may not. We may feel like we can't stand up, or we may not. We may feel heat going throughout our bodies, or we may not. Some think that if they don't experience some or all of these things, they won't be healed. But if the Word of God has been ministered to us and we receive it in faith, a seed has been sown in us that will indeed produce the desired results. An impartation of healing has been ministered to us that will bear fruit. It will come, however, in God's time.

Although it's wonderful to feel something when we are ministered to for healing, the feeling is not essential to the healing process. Feelings may or may not accompany our healing, but if faith is present, the healing will come. We can be healed without feelings, but we can't be healed without faith. (It only takes a mustard-seed faith.) We all like to feel it, but God puts the priority on the believing.

We're a sense-oriented people, and God knows that, but He also knows that faith must work outside of the senses. If we can understand and help others to understand that the healing process has begun, it will strengthen our faith and cause us never to give up hope until the victory comes.

94

Understand and Help Others to Understand That Healing Begins in the Spirit

Healing is received first in the spirit, and then it is manifested in the body. God is a spirit, and He doesn't minister to our heads; He ministers to our spirits. From there, His truths will hopefully roll over into our heads and into our senses. Then, we will be able to fully receive what He is saying.

Healing is spiritually based; so we must be spiritually healed. This is why we need to feed our spirits. The more strength and authority we have in our spirits, the more quickly we can receive our healing and the more authority we can have to resist the evil one.

This is an important point. Most people don't yet understand that their healing is spiritual, and therefore they are only looking to the flesh. If there is no change in the condition of their flesh, they accept the lie that they are not healed.

When you're ministering to someone in the healing room, look at the roots of the problem. If you focus on the physical problem the person is suffering, you will miss the spiritual root of the problem.

In the Healing Rooms, we are not a counseling service, but we need to do enough counseling to find out how the enemy has blinded the person. Then we can put the axe to the root of the thing and begin to call into manifestation the freedom that Christ paid for.

As we go forward in the healing process, truth will be added to truth ... until there is a firm foundation for healing.

Healing is always a spiritual proposition. It later manifests in the natural because we have exercised faith in our spirits. If we have more faith in the disease than we do in God's promise, we will never see the result in the flesh.

Because healing is spiritual, don't pay much attention to what is happening in the flesh. The prayer of faith will save the sick — regardless of the circumstances:

> *And the prayer of faith shall save the sick, and the Lord shall raise him up; and if he have committed sins, they shall be forgiven him.* James 5:15, KJV

As you pray for the sick, believe for a seed of faith to be sown in their spirits. Pray according to the Word of God, and actually pray the Word of God at times — word-for-word as it is recorded. This will sow a powerful seed, for the Word is seed.

Then, remember that a seed doesn't come up immediately. It has to germinate and sprout, and then you must care for the resulting plant. If you have prayed the prayer of faith, you need not look to the flesh to know if healing has occurred. Look beyond the natural, into the supernatural. Looking to the flesh will keep you sick, but looking to God will bring you healing every time.

RECOGNIZE AND HELP OTHERS TO RECOGNIZE THE WORK OF EVIL SPIRITS IN RELATIONSHIP TO HEALING

Much sickness is caused by demon spirits, and in order to recognize when a sickness is demon-related, we must minister by the Spirit. This cannot be stressed too strongly. We simply cannot perform the ministry of healing in the flesh.

If you are in the Spirit, you will often sense that a person to whom you are ministering healing has a spirit at work in him or her. Then you can take the necessary action. But first you have to know it.

For instance, I have laid hands on people and known that I was anointed, and yet the anointing seemed to bounce back at me. This is not normal, because God's intention is that the anointing we have go into the sick persons, making them whole. Usually, we can feel the sickness leaving or even see it happening. When the anointing just bounces off, we can know that we have a problem. There may be a spirit in the way preventing the person from being healed.

If this happens, we must seek God to make known to us what the spirit is, and then we must command that spirit to leave in Jesus' name. This is not child's play, and it is for these reasons, again, that we must be keen in the Spirit before we begin ministering to sick people. Learn to walk in the Spirit and hear the voice of the Spirit. There are many good teachings available on this subject, so I will not take more space in this particular book to repeat them, but this subject is vitally important.

When you are working with demon-oppressed people, don't worry so much about methods. Get in the Spirit. Only then will you be able to deal with the issues that will arise. When people adhere to only one method, they often become legalistic, and the work of the Spirit is sidelined. God doesn't always do the same thing the same way every time. Maintain the liberty of the Spirit and allow Him to work. If you become bound to a method, you will stop listening to what the Spirit says.

UNDERSTAND AND CAUSE OTHERS TO UNDERSTAND THE POWER OF THE WORD OF GOD TO HEAL

Since it is the anointing that will destroy the yoke, we must stick with what is anointed. Most importantly, God's

Word is anointed, so we always stick with His way of doing things. Depend on His Word. Use it to fight your battles. This is why we insist that those who will work in the Healing Rooms learn the Word for themselves.

If you will study the Word and hide it in your heart, the Holy Spirit will then remind you of its promises when you need a particular portion to come to mind. The Word will give you direction.

As we have said, it is impossible for us to have faith beyond our knowledge of the will of God. Knowledge of His will must come first. John recorded:

> *Then Jesus said to those Jews who believed Him, "If you abide in My word, you are My disciples indeed. And you shall know the truth, and the truth shall make you free."* John 8:31-32

Knowing the truth is what sets us free. If we don't know it, it is difficult for us to conceive of what it promises. Often we can't recognize what God is doing because we don't know what He wants to do. We have to know that a thing is possible before we can believe for it to happen to us.

Of course, the "knowing" spoken of in the Scriptures is deeper than mere mental knowing. When the Bible speaks of Adam and Eve knowing one another, it was an intimate knowing. This was not mere information; this was experience. We must know God in an intimate way, and when we do, we will not be easily deceived by the enemy.

If we allow him to do it, the enemy will deceive us, for he imitates God in many ways, trying to make us believe that night is day and day is night. But if we know God, we will not be so easily deceived. "That's not of God," we'll bluntly say. "God wouldn't do that, because I know God." It is so good to be able to say this.

When someone offers you something, purporting that it is from the Spirit, you will be able to say, "That doesn't agree with the Holy Spirit, because I know the Holy Spirit and His Word, and that isn't what the Holy Spirit is saying to me." What a great way to operate!

In politeness, we often defer to people, but God is calling us to defer to Him. If the individuals involved have the Holy Spirit living within them and they're moving in the Holy Spirit, that's one thing. If they don't, however, that's something entirely different.

Freedom from sickness comes as you and I come to know the truth. God does only what He says He will do. He does not step outside of His Word. And because of that, we need to know what it says. What God says becomes His Word, and that is what we can expect to happen.

If someone gives you "a word," make sure that it is consistent with what God has said. If it will not line up with His Word, then cast it aside. For God moves in the ways He has declared. If He has said it, we can call Him to accountability and expect Him to comply.

Jesus said:

"Heaven and earth will pass away, but My words will by no means pass away."   Matthew 24:35

God doesn't take this matter lightly. This is serious business with Him. He has personally backed His Word. That's how sure He is about what He will do for us.

Because God is that sure, we need to get into Him and gain that same assurance. Then, the devil will know who we are, because of our identification with Christ.

The psalmist declared:

99

The Children's Bread

He sent His word, and healed them,
And delivered them from their destructions.

Psalm 107:20

Know the truth, and when you know it, more faith will come to you. Knowing the will of God produces faith, and when you begin to make it known, the enemy scatters.

Speak the Word of God into those who are sick and suffering. It is not your words who will heal, but His. You may be an eloquent speaker who says wonderful things, but it will be the Word of God that will set men and women free.

Raising the Word As a Standard Against the Enemy:

We sometimes do things that open our lives up to the enemy, and he always takes advantage of these opportunities and *"comes in like a flood."* But we have the promise of the Scriptures:

When the enemy comes in like a flood,
The Spirit of the LORD will lift up a standard against
him.
Isaiah 59:19

The standard that can be raised against the enemy is the Word of God. Raise it high. Use that sword against him. He knows its power, and it is time that we do too.

We are healed by faith in the accomplishments of the cross. Let the hearing of the Word produce faith in you for healing, and then use it to produce faith in others for healing as well.

There are many things that we can choose to emphasize when we read the Bible. Some have chosen to skip over the promises related to healing, and then they wonder why they are sick. Hear what God has to say on this subject, and let His words produce faith in your heart for deliverance from every sickness.

When people come to the Healing Rooms, our work is much easier if they have had opportunity to sit under the teaching of God's Word about healing. When we lay hands on those who are prepared in this way, miracles happen much more quickly and easily.

Many of those who are opening Healing Rooms around this country and the world are also operating training programs for those who desire to have healing as a ministry. All of these ministries prefer to have helpers who are already steeped in the promises of the Word of God. It makes all the difference in the world. Nothing builds our faith like the powerful promises of God's Word.

THE WORD IS "FOREVER SETTLED":

> Forever, O LORD,
> Your word is settled in heaven.

Psalm 119:89

This is a very short verse, but it is an important one. God's Word is *"forever settled in heaven."* What does that mean? It means just what it says. It's settled. This is not a theory. A theory is sometimes only good until someone comes up with a better one.

Recently, I was listening to a radio talk show on which they were discussing dinosaurs. One of the scientists in that discussion was saying that some dinosaurs have been named which never really existed. Some bones of one animal were mistakenly joined with the bones of another, and thinking that a new creature had been discovered, the "discoverers" gave their creature a name. Later, they realized that they had just mixed the bones of two very different animals. In fact, one of the animals had not even been in the dinosaur family.

Theories are not always reliable, and we need more than theories when we stand in life-and-death situations against such a powerful enemy. This is where God's Word comes in. It is *"settled."* Like Jesus, the Word is *"the same yesterday, today, and forever"* (Hebrews 13:8). There is no variation in it, no shadow of turning. We don't have to wonder if God's going to get up tomorrow and tell us He didn't mean it after all.

God doesn't change His mind in midstream. His truths are ultimate and eternal truths. They NEVER change. Now, that's a firm foundation that we can build on. That's something real we can use against our enemy.

God's Words Are "Spirit" and "Life":

> *"It is the Spirit who gives life; the flesh profits nothing. The words that I speak to you are spirit, and they are life."*   John 6:63

The Spirit gives life because the Spirit is God. He is life, and He gives us life. Then it follows that the words the Spirit speaks to us also are *"spirit and ... life."* That's why I choose to follow God's words.

The flesh, on the other hand, *"profits nothing."* This is interesting, because most of us put far too much stock in what we are feeling at the moment, what we have been hearing, what we have been thinking. But our feelings, our thoughts and what we are hearing from others often prove to be unreliable. It is the Word of God that is *"spirit and ... life."*

This being true, we know what we need for ourselves, and we know what we need in order to minister to others. The ministry begins inside of us. We experience it first, and then we take it out to others.

Paul knew this well. He wrote:

For I am not ashamed of the gospel of Christ, for it is the power of God to salvation for everyone who believes ... .
For in it the righteousness of God is revealed from faith to faith. Romans 1:16-17

Paul refused to be ashamed of the Gospel because he knew the power of it. He was not moved when others laughed at his simplicity. He was not offended when others misunderstood his intent.

Some people will ask you, "What are you doing to get better?" and when you answer, "I'm standing on the Word of God," they will declare, "That's ridiculous."

"Well, are you any better?" they will challenge.

"Not yet," you will sometimes have to admit, "but I'm believing."

"How ridiculous!" they will sometimes say. "You need to go to a doctor." And you will have a decision to make. Are you ashamed of the promises of God? Do they seem old-fashioned and out of date to you? Trust God's promises. He never fails.

We are not against people going to doctors if they believe this is how God will heal them. We often ask the people who come to the healing rooms, "How do you believe God will heal you: by divine healing or through a doctor?" And we allow their faith to guide us. Ultimately, however, all healing comes from God, for there is no healing aside from His. What avenue you take for healing depends on your faith at the time.

Developing a Hunger for the Scriptures:

When I first came into the things of the Spirit, back in the early 1970s, I had a hunger and thirst for the Word of God that simply could not be quenched. I had little pieces of paper with the Scriptures on them that I used to memorize God's promises. I carried those little slips of paper around in my pockets. I had them pasted up all around me wherever I was. I wanted to know the Word of God by heart. I didn't want to have to pull out my Bible and look everything up, hoping against hope that I could find what I was looking for. I wanted my implements of war to be at the ready. God helped me, and within a six-month period, I was able to memorize many scriptural promises.

Even after I had memorized those promises, however, I didn't always have faith in them. I needed teaching on those passages. I needed to hear others explain them and see how they lived them. It was a growing process. Gradually, I grew in my faith as I grew in my understanding of God's Word. It is powerful to set us free and to enable us to set others free as well.

GET THE WORD INTO YOUR HEART:

The more of God's Word we can get into our hearts, the better off we will be. The wisest man of all time wrote:

> *My son, give attention to my words;*
> *Incline your ear to my sayings.*
> *Do not let them depart from your eyes;*
> *Keep them in the midst of your heart;*
> *For they are life to those who find them,*
> *And health to all their flesh.*   Proverbs 4:20-22

When you are called upon to serve in the healing ministry, go back to your notes and review them, getting all of these truths into your heart. As much as I teach these truths, they never become old to me. They are like music to my ears.

These promises from the Word of God not only help me

receive health and healing; they also strengthen and encourage my soul. What a blessing!

What was the writer saying? He was encouraging us to keep the promises of the Word of God strong within us. We must not *"let them depart."* We must *"keep them in ... [our] heart[s]."* Why? These words *"are life to those who find them."*

Although this is not often listed in the ways we can be healed, you and I can read the Bible and be healed without any other human intervention. If you read it and keep reading it, eventually you will be healed. The power and authority of the Word will cause faith to be dropped into your heart.

We have heard far too many lies from the enemy. This is why God's Word is so important. We need to pump it into our systems. *"Give attention to [it],"* *"incline your ear to [it],"* *"do not let [it] depart,"* *"keep [it] in ... your heart,"* the writer admonishes us.

This Word is *"health to [your] flesh,"* and so it must be heard, it must be received and it must be acted upon.

Sow, Expecting a Healing Harvest:

The Word is seed, and if you don't have a seed, you can't have a harvest. Sow the seed and then water it, but know that only God can give the increase. You can't will the fruit into existence.

The followers of some false cults believe that they can have something just by willing it to be so. What an arrogant belief! Who are we to will anything into existence? These men and women are gods unto themselves. Never be guilty of that error. Your will is not faith. It is God's will that we can stand on.

The anointing on God's Word destroys every yoke. Matthew recorded:

105

The Children's Bread

> *When evening had come, they brought to Him many who were demon-possessed. And He cast out the spirits with a word, and healed all who were sick, that it might be fulfilled which was spoken by Isaiah the prophet, saying:*
> *"He Himself took our infirmities and bore our sicknesses."*   Matthew 8:16-17

Even Isaiah recorded this promise in the past tense. *"He Himself TOOK our infirmities and BORE our sicknesses."* This is the Word of God, and you can base your faith on it. Jesus has already done it. He already took all our infirmities; He already bore all our sicknesses. It's done! Receive it!

If Jesus carried our sicknesses, why are we still carrying them? Many say, "I know, and I pray, but nothing seems to happen." If that's true, keep right on praying, because you are on solid ground. Don't allow the enemy to tell you that your healing is not coming. It's on the way.

The devil will do everything he can to confuse you and try to keep you from believing and receiving. He wants to get your eyes off of Jesus and His promise and onto your self and your own lack. He wants to cause you to stop shooting the arrows of the Word at him. He'll get you engaged in a serious conversation, and then he'll tell you his story — which is quite different from the truth.

David knew this secret. He wrote:

> *Your word I have hidden in my heart,*
> *That I might not sin against You.*   Psalm 119:11

What a wonderful truth!

So, we need to know the Word, and we need to sow it. Until we do, we will not have a harvest.

Moses recorded God's promise concerning *"seedtime and harvest"* in Genesis. God said:

"While the earth remains,
Seedtime and harvest,
Cold and heat,
Winter and summer,
And day and night
Shall not cease."   Genesis 8:22

The process of sowing and reaping will never fail *"while the earth remains,"* and it was still there the last time I looked.

Seeds are important, and you can't have a harvest until some of them have been planted. But if seed is planted, there will always be a harvest, and if we expect a healing to occur, we have to start planting some seeds. We can't just think about it and consider how nice it would be; we must take some action. Sow some seeds.

It's not enough to carry a whole bag of seeds around with you. Some of them have to be placed in the soil. No seed sown ... no harvest.

Once we have sown seeds, we do not expect an instant harvest. We have to cover those seeds up, walk away and leave them there in the soil — by faith that the sowing and reaping process God put in place in the beginning will not fail. For the moment, you have done your part, and you must trust that God will indeed give the increase.

We know that seeds often need additional attention. They require watering and fertilizing, weeding and culti-vating. Once a seed has been sown, we must not give up on it, forget it or neglect it. Something has to cause that seed to come up and to produce. Water it by reading the Scriptures. Feed it through prayer.

Feed the Seed of the Word Though Prayer:

The purpose of your prayers is not so much to change other people, but to change yourself. When we pray and

107

commit ourselves to God, we're saying that there's nothing we would rather do than to be in His presence and to walk and talk with Him every day. Although corporate prayer is important, private prayer is even more important for this reason.

Many things intrude upon our prayer lives, and some of them are good things in themselves. There don't seem to be enough hours in the day for family and church and community and job, but please don't neglect your relationship with God. Nothing can compare with humbling yourself in His presence. It gives you a totally different perspective on the world.

The more time you can spend alone with God, the more you will take on His righteous nature. That prevents the enemy from building a nest in your life, and that's exactly what he's looking for. He's looking for any empty place in you that he can occupy. Don't give it to him.

And if you don't open that door, he can't come in. He cannot occupy your life without your permission.

But some people get busy working for God, running here and there, doing this and that, and they fail to realize that the enemy is slowing but surely moving in. Be faithful to feed the seed you have planted with personal prayer.

God often requires that we take some action.

TAKE SOME ACTION:

God's promises can get us up from our sickbeds. Most people like to stay there until they are feeling well, but we must get up by faith. For instance, Jesus said:

> *"Therefore I say to you, whatever things you ask when you pray, believe that you receive them, and you will have them."*   Mark 11:24

What more could we ask for? *"You will have them."* You have God's word on it. Believe it and begin to do something that you could not do before.

There are times when we don't feel like doing anything at all. That's okay. Just speak the Word, and keep right on speaking it until you are better. As you speak it out, it will move from your head to your heart and begin to take effect. Healing will come forth.

Again, the promise is concerning *"whatever things you ask when you pray."* That's powerful! There is just one requirement of you: *"Believe that you receive them."* Do that, and they are yours.

Again, it's a process. Let God do it in His time, and He will do it. From the time you sow the seed to the time of the harvest, when the healing is manifested, some time might pass. That's okay. There is a process in motion that, in due time, will reach its climax.

When we know this, we will not become discouraged through waiting. If, however, we are only waiting and not watering and fertilizing the seeds that have been planted, the problems bothering us will suddenly seem to become larger and more powerful than the seeds we have sown. God said, of His promises, that they are all *"yea"* and *"Amen"* (2 Corinthians 1:20, KJV). If He said it, He will stand behind it.

Make and Teach Others to Make a Positive Confession

Confessing God's Word is an important element in the healing process. At first, we may find it difficult to actually believe what we are confessing, but as we make our confessions, the words will begin to take root in our hearts, and in time, we will begin to believe what we are confessing.

109

Satan, of course, will challenge your confession. He did it to me twice in public.

Once when I was conducting a healing service in a Pentecostal church in Germany, I began to cough so violently that I could hardly breathe. This went on until I wondered if I was going to pass out. I also felt nauseated.

What should I do? I knew that God had sent me there to bring healing to many, and I was determined not to fail them. It took me five or six minutes to get my coughing under control, but then I continued the service, and many were delivered.

This happened to me one other time. It was the very first time I had conducted a healing school, and I began to cough so badly that the young people had to come forward and pray for me. I drank some water, and the next day I was fine.

That's how the enemy works. "You fool," he taunts, "who do you think you are? What do you think you're doing?" That doesn't bother me. I know who I am (or rather, Whose I am), and I know what I'm doing.

If we back down in these moments, the enemy gains authority over us, and he will do the same thing to us again and again. However, there is more power in your life than you could ever imagine, and if you will hold steady in the moment of testing, you'll be fine.

Be careful what you confess. Your words can cancel out the effect of God's promises. When asked how they are feeling, some unwisely answer, "Oh, boy, am I sick. I feel like I'm going to die. Someone said it might be pneumonia. I don't know what it is, but I know that I'm going to have a miserable day."

Can you realize how these statements are totally contrary to what God has said? There are many ways that we need to adjust our thinking and our speaking to God's thoughts. For instance, rather than saying, "I hope I feel better," say what God says: "By His stripes, I am healed."

When you believe what God has said, you can begin to walk it out now, not wait for some future hope.

> *Let us hold fast the confession of our hope without wavering, for He who promised is faithful.*
>
> Hebrews 10:23

What is *"the confession of our hope."* Hope is a vision for the future. It's what we are putting our faith in. Our hope is in God and in what He has promised. Therefore, our *"confession of hope"* is the statement of what we're believing Him for. And we know that, through faith and patience, we inherit the promises. God is saying to us, "Hold fast."

Jesus is our hope:

> *Seeing then that we have a great High Priest who has passed through the heavens, Jesus the Son of God, let us hold fast our confession. For we do not have a High Priest who cannot sympathize with our weaknesses, but was in all points tempted as we are, yet was without sin.*
>
> Hebrews 4:14-15

This is our hope. This is our assurance. He was *"as we are,"* and yet he was *"without sin."*

Because of this, the writer continued:

> *Let us therefore come boldly to the throne of grace, that we may obtain mercy and find grace to help in time of need.* Hebrews 4:16

Because of the finished work of Calvary, you and I can now go boldly to the throne of grace and ask for help and mercy in the time of our need. It is not because we are such great children, and not at all because of our own righteousness. It is because of the righteousness of God in Christ Jesus that has been given to us. We put off our old selves and took on the Christ who now sits at the right hand of the Father.

BELIEVE IT AND THEN CONFESS IT:

Just as when we were saved, we believe in our hearts, and then we confess with our mouths. Paul wrote:

And since we have the same spirit of faith, according to what is written, "I believed and therefore I spoke," we also believe and therefore speak.   2 Corinthians 4:13

We usually speak what we believe, and it's not difficult to know where people are coming from if we listen to them long enough. What they speak is what they believe.

We have to be careful not to speak what we hear others speak if it is not in accordance with God's promises. Don't speak negatively, and if you are hearing too many negative things and this is affecting your faith, get away from it.

We need faith, and we don't need to be hearing things contrary to the Gospel. When we accepted Jesus, we accepted His finished work. If God was satisfied with the price that was paid, how can we not be satisfied with it?

MANIFEST AND TEACH OTHERS TO MANIFEST THE LOVE OF CHRIST IN EVERYTHING

We need Christ in us, and when we have something from Him, then we can begin to share it. We cannot share what we don't have in the first place. The most important thing we must share is His love.

You can't show the love of Christ if you haven't yet experienced it yourself. You can't share compassion if you have none. You cannot impart understanding if you have none to impart. You can't minister forgiveness if you haven't been forgiven.

This ministry cannot become routine or ordinary and be blessed. If we have no love for the sick, they will not be healed under our ministries. Let the mighty love that took Christ to the cross be poured out on you and your ministry today.

When you lay hands on sick men and women, it must not be just your hands. It must be the Holy Spirit moving through your hands. God will use you as a conduit, but that's all you are. He ministers through you, but it is He, in His love, who is ministering. What a privilege it is that God has taken us with all of our lacks and has placed within us a divine ability to impart His love and grace to another! What an honor!

When people are hurting, seeking healing seems like a monumental task. I feel such empathy and love for them. They need our help. They need our encouragement. They need our positiveness. They want to be healed, and God wants them to be healed, so we have a ministry to perform. Impart God's Word to them; show them His will; and, in love and compassion, believe for their deliverance.

The special circumstances of the sick demand your help. They need you to believe with them. It's easy to believe when everything is going well in life, but when you are hurting, it becomes a difficult task.

We must seek God for the love and compassion for others Jesus had when He ministered this Gospel of healing. When we look at those who are suffering, we must realize, "There, but for the grace of God, go I." I don't care how negative sick people get, we must love them and feed them the Word of God.

113

They may react badly to us because they are hurting. They may not be the most pleasant people to be around at the moment. They may not seem to be very responsive to what we are saying or doing. And we could be in their place very easily. Understand them and love them.

Don't ever look down upon a person who one day is quoting the Scriptures and the next day is down and discouraged because he or she is hurting. You don't know what you would do in that same situation. If that person can't seem to muster the necessary faith at the moment, don't be surprised or shocked by this. Just love him, and encourage him.

I often think of a time in my own life when I was suffering and in need of healing. It took me many years to get that healing, and I wondered if God would ever intervene for me. But I have found that although He doesn't always act when we want Him to, He's always right on time.

The pain and suffering I endured as a result of my sickness caused me to be in constant spiritual turmoil. In my soul, I knew what God had said on this subject, but my doctor kept telling me that I needed an operation. When I spoke with others about what I felt God's promise was, they looked at me like I was from outer space. I found it so difficult to muster any faith during those times.

Then the Holy Spirit spoke to me and said, "Get hold of yourself." It was a very real rebuke, and there was no mistaking the Lord's tone of voice. It was not frightening in any way. Actually, it tickled me and made me start to laugh.

I was eventually able to receive my healing, and that experience has made me understand what other people are feeling when they're sick and don't know what to do. I am convinced that compassion for the sick is an important key to the healing ministry.

DON'T GIVE UP, AND TEACH OTHERS
NOT TO GIVE UP

> *Therefore do not cast away your confidence, which has great reward. For you have need of endurance, so that after you have done the will of God, you may receive the promise:*
> *"For yet a little while,*
> *And He who is coming will come and will not tarry."*
>
> Hebrews 10:35-37

Don't *"cast away your confidence."* Sometimes we have confidence, and sometimes we don't. If there are other believers standing with us, we sometimes have more confidence. But just as soon as they leave, our confidence leaves with them. Stay firm in your faith. Don't give up.

This phrase *"which has great reward"* is an important one. This is true when our confidence is not in men, but in God.

There is another very important concept found in this passage: *"For you have need of endurance."* What does this have to do with the healing ministry? Because divine healing comes through a process, we need to endure until the harvest comes.

If you have been prayed for, and you felt the anointing — felt tingly all over and perhaps fell to the floor and lay there for hours (or whatever your particular experience happened to be) — and still your healing hasn't materialized, you need to go back to the Scriptures and stand on them until something does happen. It will. That's God's guarantee.

You may have received a great seed, and you knew it was from God, but unless you are willing to water and feed and cultivate it, no harvest will come. You must now stand firm against the enemy and know that God will do what He said He would do. Don't allow Satan to come back and play games with you.

115

The enemy has a plan to sow lies into your spirit. To accomplish this plan, he will send to you people who are not of faith, and they will make comments that will tend to undermine your position. He even uses well-meaning Christians. You need to make up your mind not to listen to what others say and to concentrate on the Word.

When the writer of Hebrews instructed the first-century Jewish believers: *"You have need of endurance,"* what was he referring to? He went on to say, *"So that after you have done the will of God, you may receive the promise."* What is *"the promise"*? It is the promise spoken by Isaiah: *"By His stripes we are healed"* (Isaiah 53:5).

This verse also speaks about us doing *"the will of God."* What is this *"will of God"*? It is that we would be strong and well.

DON'T EXPECT PERFECTION IMMEDIATELY:

As with salvation, believe in your heart, confess with your mouth and then begin to walk it out in real life, to establish it. But be cautious. When we first come to Christ, we sometimes don't look like we are very saved, and we sometimes don't act like we are saved. It sometimes takes a while before we look and act like we are saved. But, through experience, we now know that if we continue to walk in our salvation, the fruit of the Spirit slowly begins to appear in our lives.

We have known all along that what we need is fruit, and we are waiting to see love, peace, joy, patience, kindness, goodness, faithfulness, gentleness and self-control in our lives. But it sometimes takes a while. It isn't always apparent immediately. We know it will come, and with time and patience, it does appear.

When we receive the baptism of the Holy Spirit, we expect great power to come to us — and it does, but not always right away. We are expecting to see the gifts of the Spirit in our lives, and they come, but not always overnight.

Why is it, then, that when healing takes any time at all to manifest, we become discouraged? Is God any less trustworthy with healing than He is with the fruits of salvation or the power of the Holy Spirit baptism?

On the other hand, these experiences can come very quickly. There was a time when the ministry of healing and deliverance was thought to be so difficult that people were kept up all night or even prayed for for days on end. Now we know that this is unnecessary. God can do the work quickly and easily.

In an earlier time, some of the same views were held about receiving the baptism of the Holy Spirit. People were prayed for for many hours or days at a time. They were pulled and pushed, prodded and primed. Now we know that all of this is unnecessary. God is very willing and ready to fill us with His Spirit. All we have to do is receive.

When I sought the Holy Spirit baptism in the early 1970s, it was made so difficult that it took me a whole year to receive it. Now, we just pray and expect it to happen because we know God's will.

It also is not difficult to receive healing. The stripes were already borne by Christ on Calvary, and by His stripes we are healed. Receive your healing.

The Importance of Consistency:

Consistency is an important element of all this. We cannot be hit-or-miss Christians. Those who do special exercises only on a hit-or-miss schedule often show little progress. Those who consistently work out in a gym or on some exercise program show positive changes in their health. Nothing can replace consistency.

Stick with it. Stay the course. Remain faithful. Your healing is coming. God has promised it.

The Children's Bread

Have and Teach Others to Have
the Proper Attitude Toward Doctors and Medicines

Because we are in the healing ministry, it is important that we have the proper attitude toward doctors and medicines. We must not give them more importance than they deserve or less importance than they merit.

Many times, people do go to doctors and still don't get well. Doctors can't always help in every case. In fact, doctors can't help in many cases. Medical science, despite the fact that it has made great strides in recent decades, is still a very inexact science, and often doctors are treating our symptoms, never getting to the root of the problem. That's the wonderful thing about our Divine Physician. He understands the problem perfectly, and He can heal in every single case.

I have nothing at all against medicine, but I know that God wants to heal His children. His desire is that they be in perfect health. If some prefer to put their faith in doctors and medicines, I am not offended by that, and I stand with them in prayer. But I am trusting God, not the physicians and not the medicines. I know where the real power lies.

God may use medicines or surgery or other means for healing, but ultimately if He doesn't heal us, we cannot be healed. But we must never be guilty of "putting down" someone who comes in for prayer saying that he or she will be undergoing surgery in the near future. It is good, however, if there is some time before the surgery, to give God the opportunity to bring forth the healing. If the person's faith is for the surgery, there will be little you can do, but it doesn't hurt to try.

People are healed through the use of doctors and medicines, and we must meet them where their faith is. We must be sure, however, that all men know who the Healer is and that they give Him the glory He deserves. There is no healing apart from Him.

Doctors can sometimes tell us something to do that will speed healing, but they cannot explain to us just how that healing eventually comes. There is only one who is Almighty.

Please understand what I'm saying. If I found that I needed medicine, I would take it. But I would still believe God to heal me.

There are times when I need healing myself. Some find that difficult to understand, but I have no problem with it. Sometimes I need to get other healing ministers to stand with me in faith for my miracle. Other times, I am able to get my healing on my knees.

I never put anyone down for using medicines or doctors. I suggest that those who are on medication use those medications faithfully until they are delivered. Sometimes, in our zeal, Spirit-filled people have done some "dumb" things, and these actions have been used to poke fun at healing ministries. God wants us to be healed, and if we're not in a place where we can receive healing divinely, then we need to do what we need to do in order to walk in health — until we get ourselves to the place where we can receive divinely.

Know and Help Others to Know That We Cannot Pay for Divine Healing

We cannot pay for healing, and we cannot earn it with our good behavior. It has been freely provided for by the sacrifice of Jesus Christ, and we must simply believe and receive.

This would seem to be logical, and everyone should know it. But Naaman, like many today, wanted to pay for his healing in some way, and he couldn't. All he could do was go dip in the Jordan seven times and be humbled by the experience (see 2 Kings 5:1-14).

This is important. Pride is one of the major things that prevent people from being healed. They want to pay for something that cannot be bought. They want to merit something that cannot be merited. All that is necessary is to say, "Lord, I believe; help my unbelief."

UNDERSTAND AND HELP OTHERS TO UNDERSTAND HOW TO MAINTAIN HEALTH AND HEALING

Just like our automobiles, our bodies require maintenance. If you fail to do the required maintenance on your car and you have a problem, the manufacturer will not honor the warranty. This will result in your losing your right to make any claim for reimbursement from the manufacturer. In the same way, we are each responsible to take care of the bodies God has given to us.

This, I believe, is the purpose of God's Sabbath. He honored it and taught us that we should honor it too. If even God Almighty took a day to rest, surely we are not greater than He is, and we need to give our bodies regular rest.

Being in the ministry is no excuse for neglecting this need for physical maintenance. Ministers who become exhausted physically are often guilty of opening a door to Satan. Overtiredness brings on many maladies, and not all of them are physical.

Another challenge we have is how to maintain a healing once we have received it. This is especially difficult for those who are unsaved or spiritually immature. They often receive miraculous healings, only to lose their miracles with time.

This can also be true of those of us who have been walking for some time in the covenant. If we insist on living in sin, for example, sickness can return. We are our own worst enemies in this regard, for walking in sin opens many doors to Satan.

If our lifestyles are not conducive to good health in other respects, for instance, if we are eating improperly, not getting enough exercise or abusing drugs, we cannot expect God to keep us well. Many of those who go forward in healing crusades and receive healing continue their bad habits, and after some months or years they wind up back in the healing line. This is not the devil's fault. When looking for the enemy in these cases, take a good look in the mirror.

In the same way, if we receive healing at a conference or meeting, and we go home and fail to continue feeding our spirit man by prayer and the Word of God, our spirit, which needs healing, is starved, and we will lose our healing by default.

PRAY AND ENCOURAGE OTHERS TO PRAY SPECIAL PRAYERS

Paul's letter to the Ephesian believers contains a prayer that I have often prayed over myself and my family. I pray:

> ... that the God of our Lord Jesus Christ, the Father of glory, may give to you the spirit of wisdom and revelation in the knowledge of Him, the eyes of your understanding being enlightened; that you may know what is the hope of His calling, what are the riches of the glory of His inheritance in the saints, and what is the exceeding greatness of His power toward us who believe, according to the working of His mighty power.   Ephesians 1:17-19

This is a prayer that all those who are considering ministry to the sick and suffering, especially within one of the healing rooms, should consider praying for themselves every day for a while. As you pray this prayer, insert your own name into it, or at the very least, change "you" to "me." Make the prayer personal, and then it belongs to you.

There is another wonderful prayer in Ephesians that you should pray:

> ... that He would grant you, according to the riches of His glory, to be strengthened with might through His Spirit in the inner man, that Christ may dwell in your hearts through faith; that you, being rooted and grounded in love, may be able to comprehend with all the saints what is the width and length and depth and height — to know the love of Christ which passes knowledge; that you may be filled with all the fullness of God.
> Now to Him who is able to do exceedingly abundantly above all that we ask or think, according to the power that works in us, to Him be glory in the church by Christ Jesus to all generations, forever and ever. Amen.
>
> Ephesians 3:16-21

Again, change the "you" to "me" and the "your" to "my," and the prayer will be yours personally. If you pray prayers that are not personal, they can very quickly become mere repetition.

God hasn't finished with any of us yet, and we are still in bodies of flesh. But He is taking us from victory to victory and from glory to glory. As we walk with Him, we will eventually reach the point that we can stand on our own two feet and tell the devil where to go, in the name of the Father, Son and Holy Ghost. This will become possible to us as we consistently attend to the Word of God and its great promises for our lives.

Now, let's take a look at the role of intercessory prayer in the healing ministry.

CHAPTER FIVE

THE ROLE OF INTERCESSORY PRAYER IN HEALING

So I sought for a man among them who would MAKE A WALL, AND STAND IN THE GAP BEFORE ME on behalf of the land, that I should not destroy it; but I found no one. Ezekiel 22:30

All of those who work with us in the Healing Rooms are doing intercessory prayer. We use the term "healing technicians" to refer to those who actually administer the healing, and aside from them, we have others who do nothing but behind-the-scenes intercession. But, in actuality, we are all intercessors, for this is the ministry to which the Lord has called us.

Our intercessors pray for the technicians in the healing rooms and for those who come to receive their ministry. They are calling forth a spirit of unity among the technicians, pushing back the works of darkness and believing God for a generous flow of His anointing in the Healing Rooms. This is a vital ministry.

EVERY BELIEVER SHOULD BE AN INTERCESSOR

Every believer should be an intercessor. If we have a heart for people, we want to pray for people — whether it be in a healing room, within a group of intercessors, or in the privacy of our own homes.

An intercessor is one who stands in the gap for another, the gap between God and man, so intercessory prayer is prayer for others. In intercessory prayer, we plead for God's mercy on behalf of someone else. Intercession is never for ourselves; it is always for others.

There is nothing wrong with praying for yourself, and we all need to do it. Even Jesus prayed for Himself (see John 17). But if we only pray for ourselves, we are not fulfilling the heart of God. He calls us to bear the burdens of others, to stand in the gap for others and to see them set free and healed.

When we stand in the gap and intercede for others, it may be possible that we have never even met them, and we may not meet them this side of Heaven. By interceding on their behalf, however, we literally become a wall against the enemy to keep him from having his way in those persons' lives.

BE SENSITIVE TO GOD'S SPIRIT

As intercessors, we must be sensitive to God's Spirit. If He brings someone to your mind, you must be ready to stand in the gap for that person at that moment. The Lord will sometimes bring to your mind someone you haven't thought of in many years, and you will know that He is urging you to lift that person up before His throne of grace. That person has a need, and you can be part of his or her victory.

When my first husband was dying, it was a very terrible time for me. In my thirties and with three children, I faced an uncertain future. Worse yet, I found myself unable to share a lot of what I was experiencing with others.

Although I was a long-standing member of a prayer group, and the other members were aware, in a general sense, of our family's needs, there were times when I felt very much alone. *Nobody knows what I'm going through,* I thought, and I cried out to God in my solitude.

Later, however, one of the women in the prayer group told me that every day during that period, as she went about her daily tasks, the Lord would bring me to her mind, and she would pray for me in tongues. How merciful God is! And how wonderful it is to have others who share our heavy burdens! Surely that woman's prayers helped me to endure the difficulties of those dark days.

SOMEONE PRAYED

A close friend of mine was among those who were shot down and imprisoned in Vietnam during the war. After many other American servicemen had already been set free and repatriated, this man was still languishing in prison. All records of him had been lost, and by the time he was released, after nine long years in prison, he had become the longest-held prisoner of the entire Vietnam War.

When my friend was finally released, he was in such terrible physical condition that he required extensive medical intervention. I was eventually able to speak with him by phone, and he told me that he had been kept in a tiny bamboo cubicle barely large enough to lie down in, and that the prison guards had harassed him terribly.

"How were you able to bear it?" I asked him.

"One night," he said, "I thought to myself, *I can't go on.* I had already suffered through more than eight years of unspeakable horrors by then. *I can't go on, and I don't want to go on. This is the end.* I spoke to God and said to Him, 'Take my life; just take my life. Please, don't let me have to go on like this any more. I can't take it.'

THE CHILDREN'S BREAD

"Then, all of a sudden, a light shone in that pitch-black bamboo cell. That light stayed on me all night, and when the light from outside began to come in that next morning, I knew that I was going to make it ... I was going to survive. That experience sustained me through the next nine months until I was released and repatriated."

We may never know who, but I am sure that someone somewhere was praying for my friend the night he experienced his darkest trial, and whoever it was prayed with such diligence that God heard his or her cry. That person interceded with so much faith on this friend's behalf that God ministered to him in that very supernatural way.

COUNT IT A PRIVILEGE

When God gives you an opportunity to intercede for someone, count it a real privilege. As you pray for other people, you are experiencing the highest form of God's love poured out through your heart. And the more you pray for others, the more you will be blessed yourself.

Praying for others is an actual form of praise, for by doing this you are recognizing the grace of God upon your own life and being grateful enough to share it with someone else — known or unknown. How wonderful!

Intercessory prayer is also spiritual warfare; it is the battlefield of prayer. Stand guard and do battle for those whom God lays upon your heart.

Job said something very powerful that bears careful examination:

> "To him who is afflicted, kindness should be shown by his friend,
> Even though he forsakes the fear of the Almighty."
> Job 6:14

This is an amazing statement when you consider the condition Job was in when he spoke these words. He had been going through some terrible trials of his own. They were so terrible that each day must have seemed like a lifetime.

Job's Revelation

During this time, each of Job's friends had his own idea about what Job had to do to get his life straightened out. Job wasn't sure that any of these ideas was valid, but he was sure that no one deserved the treatment that he was receiving — *"even,"* he said, if *"he forsakes the fear of the Almighty."*

This is remarkable. Job was not insisting, as most of us do, that men deserve what comes to them; he was recognizing the need to say, "There, but for the grace of God, go I." We are very good at judging what others are going through and what they should do ... until we stand in their shoes and have to do it for ourselves. Then the view seems very different. If we could only get more in touch with our own humanity, we would be much better intercessors. We would understand why people suffer and know why they need our help.

I wonder how many of us were saved because of a praying mother or grandmother or someone else we didn't even know about who was praying for us at the time. It would be interesting to know.

Jesus interceded for Peter, and it is good for us to examine just how He prayed:

And the Lord said, "Simon, Simon! Indeed, Satan has asked for you, that he may sift you as wheat. But I have

The Children's Bread

*prayed for you, that your faith should not fail; and when
you have returned to Me, strengthen your brethren."*
Luke 22:31-32

When we go through some difficulty and the Lord saves
us out of the hand of the enemy, we are strengthened to
share with others. So, just as others have helped us in our
times of crises, we must now dedicate ourselves to help
others in their times of need. There is not one of us who
could not point to a moment in time when the prayers of
some other person somewhere kept us from going under.
Can we now do any less for others?

When you pray for others, you lose nothing, and you
gain everything. You would not be better off just praying
for yourself. Maturity demands that you look beyond yourself, and when you enter into intercession, you are sowing
seeds that will surely be reaped in your own life. At the
very least, your life will be enriched by your experience of
selfless intercession.

Never Give Up on Anyone

We must never limit God, and we must never give up
on anyone. As long as there is life, there is hope, and as the
old saying goes, "It ain't over till it's over." Keep praying.
Your intercessory prayer on behalf of another can reverse
that person's situation.

My Baptist uncle, who is nearly a hundred years old
now, was for many years pastor of First Baptist Church in
Memphis, Tennessee. He spoke to standing-room-only au-
diences in Moscow back before that was commonly done.
He has written many books, was a professor of Greek at a
Baptist seminary for many years and uses only his Greek
New Testament.

After I received the things of the Spirit, I asked him what he thought about speaking in tongues and the gifts of the Spirit. "I know it's in the Bible," he said, "and I know that some people receive that gift." Then he asked, "Are you suggesting that I don't have the Holy Spirit because I don't speak in tongues?"

"Not at all," I told him, "but I do wonder if you fully understand the power of the Holy Spirit."

"Well, let me tell you a story," he said, and he proceeded to do just that. A lady in his church had a wayward son for whom she had long prayed. The more she prayed, the worse her son seemed to get. One night she called my uncle in the middle of the night and asked him to come to the hospital because her son had been involved in a motorcycle accident. My praying uncle got up, got dressed and went to the hospital.

When he arrived at the hospital, he found that the young man had already died. He asked a nurse where the mother was, and she showed him into a private family room. There the woman was on her knees crying out to God. "But Father, You promised me. You promised me You wouldn't take him home until he was saved." She kept repeating this over and over.

As my uncle witnessed this, his heart was broken, and he, too, dropped to his knees and began to cry out to the Father along with the desperate mother. Together, they prayed for some forty-five minutes.

Then, suddenly, the door opened, and a nurse rushed in to say that there had been a mistake. The boy was alive after all. This happened with those who didn't yet seem to understand the workings of the Holy Spirit, and how much more God can do such things through those who know His fullness.

When I didn't seem to be surprised by this, my uncle

went on to tell me another story. He had suffered with sickness in his own body, and when he had done everything he knew to get well, he still wasn't feeling any better. After this had gone on for a while, one night he became very discouraged. Before he went to bed that night, he got down on his knees by the side of his bed and cried out to God. "Father, I can't hold on much longer. I desperately need healing in my body. I can't help myself, and the doctors can't seem to help me either. You are my only hope." He went to bed and awoke the next morning completely healed.

Don't be influenced in your intercession by a person's experience or lack of experience. God wants to do many things for us that we miss because our lack of faith holds Him back. When He urges your spirit to pray, don't miss the opportunity for any reason.

GOD CAN DO THE IMPOSSIBLE

One summer I read that food was not getting into North Korea, where the people were experiencing a terrible famine, and that many older people and babies were suffering and dying as a result. Stories of people resorting to cannibalism had even surfaced. I could somehow see those older people and hear those babies crying for food. "Lord," I prayed, "let me make a difference in this situation," and I made a commitment to pray for the starving people of North Korea until food was available in abundance.

I began praying in June, and although no more news articles appeared in our local new media about food shortages in North Korea, I continued my intercession throughout the summer. In September, another article appeared, saying that food was now getting through to North Korea. Although I'm sure that others accepted the call to pray for the people of North Korea and that I was not the only one, I also know that my prayers did make a difference in that nation and its peoples.

ONE PERSON CAN AFFECT THOUSANDS OF OTHERS

One person can affect the lives of thousands of others through intercessory prayer:

> *Five of you shall chase a hundred, and a hundred of you*
> *shall put ten thousand to flight;*
> *your enemies shall fall by the sword before you.*
> Leviticus 26:8

God is raising up an army of intercessors, and you and I can be part of that army. In this way, we become partners with Him.

He has shown us that nothing is too hard for Him:

> *"Behold, I am the LORD, the God of all flesh. Is there*
> *anything too hard for Me?"*   Jeremiah 32:27

When the Spirit of God places a burden upon your heart, know that it *is* possible. God will not direct you to intercede for something that cannot be accomplished.

We are called to *"bear one another's burdens."* This, the Scriptures declare, *"fulfill[s] the law of Christ"*:

> *Bear one another's burdens, and so fulfill the law of*
> *Christ.*   Galatians 6:2

With the importance and power of intercessory prayer now established, let me state briefly some things that are important for you to remember in regard to intercessory prayer.

The Children's Bread

Enter God's Presence With Worship

Begin every prayer with praise and worship. As David showed us in the Psalms, this is the proper way to enter into God's presence:

Enter into His gates with thanksgiving,
And into His courts with praise.
Be thankful to Him, and bless His name.
For the Lord is good;
His mercy is everlasting,
And His truth endures to all generations.

Psalm 100:4-5

Many of us rush into God's presence waving our list of demands before Him, and this is not the proper way to approach our Creator and Benefactor. If we would spend more time in praise and worship, we could make fewer requests of Him. Many of our needs would be automatically supplied.

Praise and worship also have a faith-building element to them. As you remember all the good things that God has already done for you and you thank Him for them, your faith in His ability to do everything else you need Him to do will increase.

When I get on my knees before God, the first thing I want to do is to let Him know how wonderful He is. He is the Mighty One who loves me with an everlasting love. I want to thank Him for caring for me, for providing all of my needs. He is the Most Glorious One.

I thank God for the sunshine of each morning and the beauty of the day. I thank God for the birds that I hear chirping. I thank Him that I am still breathing, that my legs still work and that I can still see. I thank Him for the people He has placed in my life and for the love we share.

To some, this may sound like little Sunday school children talking to God, but we need to regain that childlike faith and gratitude for life. The more you enter into His gates with thanksgiving and into His courts with praise, the more you will become convinced that nothing is impossible for you, that nothing can prevent your prayers from being answered.

PRAY SPECIFICALLY

Be specific, not vague, when you pray. Don't major in minors, but rather major in the power of God, His authority and His faithfulness to His plan.

Jesus said:

> *"And whatever you ask in My name, that will I do, that the Father may be glorified in the Son."* John 14:13

The promise is *"whatever you ask,"* so be specific. Don't pray only in generalities.

Sometimes, when we ask those who come into the Healing Rooms what their problems are, what they want us to pray about, they say they don't know. When this happens, we look on the forms they fill out when they arrive to see if they have stated some more specific needs there. We need something to focus our prayers around. Otherwise, how will we know if God has answered?

Jesus had a habit of asking people a question when He met them in their need: "Do you want to be healed?" It seems like a strange question. When people are hurting, of course they want to be healed. At least that's the way we think. But Jesus knew that not everyone wanted to be healed badly enough to believe Him and receive.

Often when we ask people who come for prayer, "What is your need?" they don't seem to be sure of just what they are seeking. Perhaps they are not sure what is available and what is not. Often we must help people understand the proper goal, the right need, the correct target for their prayers. This is important, for they will receive nothing more than the target they have in their minds, nothing more than they ask for.

If people do not have a precise goal in mind, how can they possibly reach it? They have nothing to reach for, nothing for which to put their faith into motion. And many have not yet put their faith into motion precisely because they have not yet set a goal they wish to attain. A goal is something we are hoping for, something we have envisioned, and such a vision is vital to faith.

When people have no purpose, no reason for living, they easily fall into depression. They easily lose hope. As someone has said, "Their get-up-and-go has done got up and went." This is not unusual, and we must help people to, once again, find a worthy goal, have an inspired vision, possess a divine hope.

When we ask people what they want, they should know immediately, and then we can agree with them in prayer. We need to know God's promises concerning prayer and the power of agreement, and then we can encourage those to whom we minister that they can receive anything and everything they need and want in God.

BE MOTIVATED BY LOVE

For in Christ Jesus neither circumcision nor uncircumcision avails anything, but faith working through love.
Galatians 5:6

Faith works by love. When your love factor is high, your faith will also be high. But when your love factor is down, you will have a hard time mustering enough faith for effective intercessory prayer. Let God's love flow through you as you pray.

Job was restored when he prayed for his friends (see Job 42:10). He had to forgive them for their bad attitudes and their "bright ideas," and he had to love them. Then, his intercessory prayer for them was answered, and he himself was restored.

Jesus taught very strongly on this subject:

"For if you forgive men their trespasses, your heavenly Father will also forgive you. But if you do not forgive men their trespasses, neither will your Father forgive your trespasses."   Matthew 6:14-15

God is looking for the pure in heart, and their purity will keep them out of the hospital and out of the doctor's office. Ask God to show you what is hindering your prayers, as Paul prayed for the Ephesians, *"the eyes of your understanding being enlightened"* (Ephesians 1:18).

What hinders you may not be what hinders another, for each of us has a different weakness. Learn what most often hinders you, and then fight it.

Most of us are good at detecting the faults of others but not our own. God's Word instructs us to concentrate on our own weaknesses, and not be overly concerned with the weaknesses of others. Jesus taught:

"And why do you look at the speck in your brother's eye, but do not consider the plank in your own eye? Or how can you say to your brother, 'Let me remove the speck from your eye'; and look, a plank is in your own

135

eye? Hypocrite! First remove the plank from your own eye, and then you will see clearly to remove the speck from your brother's eye."   Matthew 7:3-5

Tend to your own business first and foremost, allowing the Holy Spirit to instruct you, and then God will use you to bless others.

Jesus left us with *"a new commandment"*:

"A new commandment I give to you, that you love one another; as I have loved you, that you also love one another. By this all will know that you are My disciples, if you have love for one another."   John 13:34-35

Nothing is more important than love. This is our secret of success. Since love never fails, love in us will also cause us never to fail.

When all else fails, love the people to whom you are ministering. If you can't think of another prayer to pray for them, love them. Love is powerful.

When my brother died in an automobile accident, his young son was devastated. He had loved his Daddy so much. He moped around the house and didn't eat well for some time afterward.

I went to visit the family, and when I saw what was happening to that boy, my heart broke. I asked his mother if I could take him home and keep him for a while, and she agreed. That year I had an eight-year-old with me all summer, and we did many great things together. During that time, the boy gained twelve pounds, and his mother was amazed when she saw him getting off the plane coming back home.

But it hadn't been all that easy. He would often wake up during the night and I would find him wandering around the house. He would say to me, "Aunt Lanie, my Daddy's dead."

"Honey," I would say, "I know."

Sometimes there were no words to comfort him. How do you explain such a loss to an eight-year-old? I would sit down on the floor and take him in my arms, and we would cry together.

Sometimes there's nothing else that we know to do, but love can do what we cannot. By the end of summer, that boy's grief was healed. He still loved and missed and talked about his Daddy, but he was ready to get on with life.

Sometimes people are suffering such grief that they can't get past it. They're stuck. In these cases, only love will be the balm they so desperately need.

It's not always a great prayer that is needed. Sometimes you just need to hold someone's hand. You might want to admit to the person, "I care about what you're going through. I really don't know what I can say or do to give you peace, but I want you to know that I love you and that I'm here for you." That's enough many times.

Everyone needs love, and many members of the Body of Christ are starved for it. A touch, a handclasp, a hug, a kiss ... these are all powerful therapies for those who are hurting. We need to express our appreciation more for those we love and appreciate: "You really made my day." "I'm moved and comforted by your faith. I love to see you coming, and I love to hear your voice. I'm so blessed by your presence."

I am very blessed to be loved by my husband. That may sound odd to some, but it is a great comfort to be genuinely loved. Bud prays for me, and I never take his love for granted. What a wonderful gift he is to me!

When we feel the need for love ourselves, it is time for

us to sow love to others. If you sow love, you will reap a harvest of love for yourself.

DRAW ON THE SPIRIT'S UNLIMITED KNOWLEDGE AND WISDOM

Our modern computer databases are truly amazing. We type in a word representing a subject, and up comes a list of available resources for that desired subject. The Holy Spirit is much more knowledgable than all of the computerized information available to us. Get plugged into Him, and He will reveal truth to you.

These days we have so much information available to us that it is often difficult to wade through all of it and find what we are looking for. The Holy Spirit can show you exactly what you need to know in an instant's time.

NEVER PRESUME UPON GOD

Presumption is foolish, especially if that presumption is based on some past experience. God doesn't always do things the same way every time. In each case, He chooses how He will act. This in not our choice. Look to God, not to experience.

When we expect things to happen always in a prescribed way, we will surely be disappointed. Experience, our senses and the way people are reacting are not valid signposts to help us determine whether God is or isn't moving. He is the rewarder of our faith, not of our feelings.

If we expect God to work in a certain way always, we tie His hands. Let Him be God.

PRAY WITH FAITH

But without faith it is impossible to please Him [God],

The Role of Intercessory Prayer in Healing

for he who comes to God must believe that He is, and that He is a rewarder of those who diligently seek Him.
Hebrews 11:6

This is part of the reason that God often requires us to come to Him again and again before He answers. He wants to see that we really believe Him and that our faith does not fail.

Pray With Fervor

Some people pray, but not fervently, about healing for a particular sickness ... until they become seriously ill themselves. Then they get serious in prayer, and they immediately receive healing.

Desperation often benefits our prayers, causing them to be more fervent. Let us pray fervently for others, although we may have difficulty feeling what they are feeling and sensing what they are sensing. Let the Spirit place the urgency for prayer into your heart.

Pray in the Spirit

Likewise the Spirit also helps in our weaknesses. For we do not know what we should pray for as we ought, but the Spirit Himself makes intercession for us with groanings which cannot be uttered. Romans 8:26

We have touched upon many of these other themes elsewhere, so I am compelled to dwell more at length on this very important subject. *"We do not know what we should pray for,"* but the Holy Ghost does. It makes sense, therefore, to depend on His help in intercessory prayer.

Those who speak in tongues have a great advantage in

this regard. Often, when we don't know what we should say in prayer, the Spirit takes over and prays through us. This is what the Scriptures call *"praying in the Holy Spirit"* (Jude 20).

When the Spirit is working through us, we have *"rivers of living water"* flowing from our innermost being (John 7:38). What could be more wonderful?

When we are praying for a spouse or for a child or even for others, there are some general things that we can always ask for. We can ask the Lord to protect our spouses, for example, to keep them safe, to bless them in their endeavors, to give them wisdom to deal with particular situations. There are also some very specific requests that we can make for others relating to the particular events of the day. But when we have exhausted the list of our perceived needs, it's time to pray in the Spirit and allow Him to express the needs we cannot know about or understand.

When praying for spouses and children, we sometimes tend to get in the flesh. After all, we know these individuals very well, and our feelings may become involved. This is another reason it is good to pray in the Spirit. In our flesh, we sometimes pray for things we think God needs to be doing, but our prayers may only be addressing the symptoms of the problem, not the source. We may even finish our prayers without having hit on the real need. If we pray in the Spirit (in tongues), He will pray the truth and give attention to the real need.

Praying in the Spirit builds faith:

> *But you, beloved, building yourselves up on your most holy faith, praying in the Holy Spirit ...*   Jude 20

When you find that you cannot pray loving things about people, the best thing you can do is pray for them in the

Spirit. When others have been unkind to you, ask God to show you what made them act or speak that way. Intercede for them that they will be ministered to in their spirits. Free them (loose them) from guilt because of the way they have treated you, so that they might be blessed. When you loose others, you also loose yourself. Then pray the rest in the Spirit.

Praying in the Spirit is edifying to oneself:

He who speaks in a tongue edifies himself.
1 Corinthians 14:4

Paul spent several chapters in his first letter to the Corinthian believers describing the various uses of speaking in tongues and what is accomplished by each. One use of speaking in tongues, for instance, is a message to the church, and since we don't understand it, we need it to be accompanied by interpretation. Another use for speaking in tongues, Paul showed, is to pray in the Spirit.

If your spirit is weak, pray in tongues more. If your faith is weak, pray in tongues more. This is a direct way to receive strength from God. Those who need healing would do well to pray more in the Spirit. If you have a difficult question you want God to answer, pray more in tongues. If you have a difficult situation you want God to resolve, pray more in tongues. Anything you can do to build up your spirit cannot hurt you, and this is one of the easiest ways to do it.

As you pray in the Spirit, your spirit is being fed, and you are exercising your spirit. If you have never spoken in tongues, find someone who can help you receive this experience. It is so important that we require it in all those who work in the Healing Rooms.

We have nothing against those who are not yet Spirit-filled. We love them, and they are God's children too. But this experience, which we commonly call the baptism of the Holy Spirit, is an experience that we all need in order to have power to work for God.

Just before going back to Heaven, Jesus commanded His disciples to wait in Jerusalem until they had been endued with power from on high:

> *"Behold, I send the Promise of My Father upon you; but tarry in the city of Jerusalem until you are endued with power from on high."*　　　　Luke 24:49

When Paul encountered a group of men who were disciples of John the Baptist, he asked them:

> *Have ye received the Holy Ghost since ye believed?*
> 　　　　　　　　　　　　　　Acts 19:2, KJV

What they answered him was absolutely amazing:

> *We have not so much as heard whether there be any Holy Ghost.*　　　　　　　　　　Acts 19:2, KJV

This is the problem. Many have not yet known about this wonderful experience. They confuse it with John's baptism for repentance or Jesus' baptism of forgiveness. This is a totally different experience, but it is likened to water baptism because when it happens, we are immersed in the Spirit. The Spirit is in us, and we are in the Spirit.

Repentance is important and forgiveness is important, but being filled with the Spirit is also important to every believer. And speaking in tongues is the evidence of that baptism.

This experience will change your life dramatically. Take

it from an old Baptist girl who wouldn't have been caught dead speaking in tongues when she was growing up. Now I thank God for this experience, because it has changed my life.

PRAY IN THE NAME OF JESUS

"And in that day you will ask Me nothing. Most assuredly, I say to you, whatever you ask the Father IN MY NAME He will give you. Until now you have asked nothing IN MY NAME. Ask, and you will receive, that your joy may be full." John 16:23-24

This is the secret to full joy: asking, and receiving what we ask for. Do it in the name of Jesus, for His name is powerful:

He was clothed with a robe dipped in blood, and His name is called The Word of God. Revelation 19:13

I love this verse. It puts goose bumps on top of my goose bumps. Jesus is clothed with a robe dipped in blood, and of course, that blood represents our freedom and our hope of eternal life. All of our needs are met *"according to His [God's] riches in glory by Christ Jesus"* (Philippians 4:19). It is by His stripes that we were healed, because He is our Deliverer and our Defender. Let us boldly use the authority of His name:

"And whatever you ask in My name, that I will do, that the Father may be glorified in the Son. If you ask anything IN MY NAME, I will do it." John 14:13-14

"You did not choose Me, but I chose you and appointed you that you should go and bear fruit, and that your

fruit should remain, that whatever you ask the Father
IN MY NAME He may give you."　　　John 15:16

When you approach the Father, do it in the authority of the name of Jesus. That will get you into the throne room. That will cause you to be heard. This name is above every other name.

You can come boldly in His name. You can ask largely in His name. His name is your password to riches. This is a ticket that never expires and never goes out-of-date. Just as He is, His name is *"the same yesterday, today, and forever."*

There is only one name to which the enemy will bow, and it's certainly not yours or mine. Satan won't bow to us, but he will bow to Jesus. He won't bow to the name of the most important and well-known minister of our day or even to the name of the most famous and powerful preacher of all times. He won't bow to the name of a church or of a particular religious organization. He won't bow to the name of a large corporation or one of its managers. We cannot emphasize this truth too much; our enemy will only bow to the name of Jesus and only when we use that name in faith.

Pray With Patience

But those who wait on the Lord
Shall renew their strength;
They shall mount up with wings like eagles,
They shall run and not be weary,
They shall walk and not faint.　　　Isaiah 40:31

Waiting, being patient, is not easy, and most of us have a problem with it. But things happen in God's time, and there is no way we can change that.

We want what we want when we want it. We want things to happen right now, or better yet, "yesterday." But impatience will surely lead to further delays. When we get in a hurry, we begin to make mistakes. We can't get the keys out of the door. Then we drop them. We spill things on ourselves. There is no replacement for patience.

> *Imitate those who THROUGH FAITH AND PATIENCE inherit the promises.*   Hebrews 6:12

The combination of faith and patience is powerful and causes us to *"inherit the promises."* Even Jesus had to learn endurance:

> *... looking unto Jesus, the author and finisher of our faith, who for the joy that was set before Him ENDURED the cross, despising the shame, and has sat down at the right hand of the throne of God. For consider Him who ENDURED such hostility from sinners against Himself, lest you become weary and discouraged in your souls.*
> Hebrews 12:2-3

Waiting shows endurance. It shows maturity. It shows that we are no longer impetuous. And the waiting serves more than one purpose. It gives us time to think, to sort things out, to clear our minds. It gives us time to sift the chaff from the wheat, and have the things that are hindering us blown away by the Spirit. Don't rush God:

> *Woe to those who draw iniquity with cords of vanity,*
> *And sin as if with a cart rope;*
> *That say, "Let Him [God] make speed and hasten His work,*
> *That we may see it."*   Isaiah 5:18-19

145

"Woe" to them. We cannot afford to rush God. He may not come when we want Him to, but He's always on time. He knows the best moment to reveal Himself.

The children of Israel had to remain in the wilderness for many years, but this wasn't God's fault. He had to wait for them to grow up. Waiting brings maturity and settles many issues. Waiting is a demonstration of faith.

Having to wait seems deadly for many. They forget what they were believing for. They give up hope of ever receiving an answer.

Don't lay down any prayer the Spirit has placed upon your heart. It will come to pass, if not today, then in God's tomorrow. God hasn't forgotten His promises, and you must not either. He is the same yesterday, and today, and forever. We forget, but He never does.

The wise Solomon, in his writings in Ecclesiastes, showed us that there is a time for everything:

> *To everything there is a season,*
> *A time for every purpose under heaven:*
> *A time to be born,*
> *And a time to die;*
> *A time to plant,*
> *And a time to pluck what is planted ... ..*
>
> Ecclesiastes 3:1-2

We know that God makes all things beautiful in their time (see Ecclesiastes 3:11).

When a woman is expecting a child, we know to anticipate its birth in about nine months, but not every child comes on a given day. Doctors, therefore, give a mother a range of days during which the child might be born. Apart from inducing the birth, she has no choice but to be patient and to allow the child to come in its own time. God holds

146

in His hand the timing of births and deaths, and everything else in between.

We must make a decision. Either we believe God and
we can wait for His timing, or we don't believe Him and
we move on to other things.

God knows when we are ready for the answers to our
prayers. Many times He is preparing us, and when we are
ready, He is ready. We need some experiences along the
way. Stop concentrating on how long it is taking you to
receive an answer to your prayers, and start concentrating
on what it is God is about to do. Get ready for it.

Concerning prayer, Jesus said:

> *"Ask, and it will be given to you; seek, and you will find;*
> *knock, and it will be opened to you. For everyone who*
> *asks receives, and he who seeks finds, and to him who*
> *knocks it will be opened."*   Matthew 7:7-8

These verbs *"ask," "seek"* and *"knock"* are all in a pro-
gressive tense. They mean, "ask and keep on asking, seek
and keep on seeking and knock and keep on knocking."
Don't grow weary in well doing. Keep on keeping on. Don't
give up. Don't let the enemy rob you. Allow God to mature you and prepare you and do through you what He
desires to be done.

Jeremiah spoke on God's behalf:

> *"Call to Me, and I will answer you, and show you great*
> *and mighty things, which you do not know."*
>   Jeremiah 33:3

Waiting upon the Lord produces an increase in our expectations, and if we believe what God is saying, waiting
will not be nearly as difficult. He will show us *"great and*

mighty things." That sounds like things beyond our imagination. Waiting produces such expectations.

As we have seen, healing is a process that takes time. Don't be impatient, and don't rush God. He knows exactly what He's doing. Ask Him about the proper timing.

Don't Be Afraid to Ask God Questions

Children learn so very much during their first years of life because they ask many questions. They ask "why" about everything:

"Why is the sky blue?"

"Why does the sun go down?"

"Why does it rain?"

"Why ...?"

"Why ... ?"

At the time, these many questions often seem irritating, but how are we to learn unless we ask. James wrote to the churches, *"You do not have because you do not ask"* (James 4:2).

Jesus loves it when we come to Him as little children, stop pretending that we know everything and are all grown up and start asking Him about everything. He is the Head, and we are the body, and how will the body know what to do if it doesn't ask the Head?

Stop trusting what everyone else is saying at the moment, and ask Him what He thinks about a given subject. Learn His strategy. Ask Him to show you what the enemy is up to. Let Him give you discernment in every situation.

One day a Canaanite woman came to Jesus with a plea for her demon-possessed child. At first, the Lord's answer did not seem to be positive, but she persevered and received the answer she sought:

> *Then Jesus went out from there and departed to the region of Tyre and Sidon. And behold, a woman of Canaan*

came from that region and cried out to Him, saying, "Have mercy on me, O Lord, Son of David! My daughter is severely demon-possessed."

But He answered her not a word.

And His disciples came and urged Him, saying, "Send her away, for she cries out after us."

But He answered and said, "I was not sent except to the lost sheep of the house of Israel."

Then she came and worshiped Him, saying, "Lord, help me!"

But He answered and said, "It is not good to take the children's bread and throw it to the little dogs."

And she said, "Yes, Lord, yet even the little dogs eat the crumbs which fall from their masters' table."

Then Jesus answered and said to her, "O woman, great is your faith! Let it be to you as you desire." And her daughter was healed from that very hour.

Matthew 15:21-28

What do you do when you think God is saying "No" to your prayer? This woman was wise. She got closer to Him and worshiped Him.

If you think He is saying "No," ask Him why. Tell Him you love Him and that you are asking because of one of His promises. Worship Him and draw near to Him. That may be just what He is looking for.

When Jesus seemed to be saying "No" to this woman, it didn't discourage her. It just set her faith in motion. Don't quit praying when you fail to understand what God is doing. Hold on, and you will learn the whys of His delays. Then, persevere until the answer comes.

A working knowledge of intercessory prayer is essential to ministry in the healing rooms. When we know how to intercede in prayer, we will not be discouraged when things do not seem to be going our way. Prayers of faith give us patience, and this is something we need to be reminded of again and again.

LISTEN TO WHAT GOD IS SAYING IN RESPONSE

Sometimes the delays we suffer in receiving answers to our prayers may be caused by our not hearing what God is saying about a particular case. We are often so busy asking Him to heal a person that we don't take time to listen to what He is telling us. Part of our prayer time must be speaking, but another part must be spent in listening. How else will we receive an answer?

> *Then He said, "Go out, and stand on the mountain before the LORD." And behold, the LORD passed by, and a great and strong wind tore into the mountains and broke the rocks in pieces before the LORD, but the LORD was not in the wind; and after the wind an earthquake, but the LORD was not in the earthquake; and after the earthquake a fire, but the LORD was not in the fire; and after the fire a still small voice.*
> *So it was, when Elijah heard it, that he wrapped his face in his mantle and went out and stood in the entrance of the cave. Suddenly a voice came to him, and said, "What are you doing here, Elijah?"*   1 Kings 19:11-13

Sometimes we are busy looking for the spectacular to happen, but God is speaking in *"a still small voice."* If He speaks in this way, then we must be still in order to hear what He is saying to us. Many of us are good at the speech part, but we are poor at the listening. We must learn the art of listening, and be patient as we listen, knowing that if we ask God a question, He will answer.

The Role of Intercessory Prayer in Healing

Get a Biblical Perspective on Satan

When you look at Satan in prayer, see him through the eyes of God. Don't think in relationship to something terrible he has done. He only has power as God gives it to him for an intended and specific purpose. In reality, he is quite frail and weak. He cannot do anything that God does not permit him to do.

Satan wants to make us afraid of him, but if we will ask God to show us who Satan really is, we will no longer fear him. Don't ask Satan's opinion, because he will surely tell you a lie. And don't ask some other person's opinion. Ask God. Say to Him, "Show me how You see Satan." When He does, all fear of the enemy will be removed.

> *"How you are fallen from heaven,*
> *O Lucifer, son of the morning!*
> *How you are cut down to the ground,*
> *You who weakened the nations!*
> *For you have said in your heart:*
> *'I will ascend into heaven,*
> *I will exalt my throne above the stars of God;*
> *I will also sit on the mount of the congregation*
> *On the farthest sides of the north;*
> *I will ascend above the heights of the clouds,*
> *I will be like the Most High.' "*   Isaiah 14:12-14

This is how Satan talks. He is the most audacious liar, the father of lies. But what does God have to say about him?

> *"Yet you shall be brought down to Sheol,*
> *To the lowest depths of the Pit.*
> *Those who see you will gaze at you,*
> *And consider you, saying:*

151

'Is this the man who made the earth tremble,
Who shook kingdoms,
Who made the world as a wilderness
And destroyed its cities,
Who did not open the house of his prisoners?' "

Isaiah 14:15-17

You see, God is far greater than the bluffing Satan. The time will come when all the world will see him for what he is. Until that time, we can surely go before the throne of grace and say, "Father, help me to see Satan through Your eyes, so that I will not be shaken by his lies. Let me see that You are the Creator, and that there's nothing impossible with You. Confirm to my heart that Satan is simply an imitator and not even a good one at that. He tries so hard to make himself look big, but You can 'take him out' anytime You want to."

God has a plan and a purpose, and that includes a purpose for Satan. When the devil's time of usefulness to God is ended, he will be bound in chains for all eternity. Until that time, God is using him to prove all men, to separate the sheep from the goats. Satan presents an alternative, so that men have the choice to believe him or to accept Christ and not be lost for all eternity.

Occasionally we meet a person who feels that Satan is so evil, so mean and ugly, that no one can fight him. But this is often just a bluff. The goodness of God is able to bring every man to repentance, and God is patiently working on the soul of every man. He could have said, "Wipe them out because I'm sick and tired of looking at them," but His great love prevented Him from doing that.

God is the great Creator, and all things are possible with Him. He has given us great promises:

THE ROLE OF INTERCESSORY PRAYER IN HEALING

Now this is the confidence that we have in Him, that if
we ask anything according to His will, He hears us. And
if we know that He hears us, whatever we ask, we know
that we have the petitions that we have asked of Him.

1 John 5:14-15

On the basis of those promises, don't back down —
whatever the circumstances seem to be. Satan doesn't have
any corner on the market. His rights are very limited. Was
he there when God created all things? If he was there in
any part of the Creation, he certainly had no say in it. He
couldn't have done it himself, and he had no right to inter-
fere. Our God is greater:

You are of God, little children, and have overcome them,
because He who is in you is greater than he who is in
the world.   1 John 4:4

If you doubt it at any time, ask the Father to let you see
the truth. Ask Him to open your eyes to see into the heavenly realms.

Not long ago I was awakened one night by the presence
of someone standing beside my bed. I thought Bud must
have gone to the bathroom and lost his way getting back
to the bed in the dark, but then I opened my eyes and
quickly realized that this was no man. He was a horrible
looking creature, gnarly and warty, with some type of icky
green substance all over his face. He was dressed in a hood
and cape, and he was standing over me shaking his finger
at me in a threatening fashion.

I knew immediately that this was God's answer to my
prayers to see more into the world of evil spirits. I rolled
over onto my other side and went back to sleep. I wasn't
about to allow that wicked creature to rob me of my rest.

153

THE CHILDREN'S BREAD

The next day Bud and I prayed about why this happened. It had been a shock, but I was so glad that I had not been afraid. I realized that I was seeing the demon through the Lord's eyes, and he was nothing more than a Halloween character.

If I had seen that same thing through my own eyes, I would no doubt have been shaking in my boots. God was gracious to allow me to see into the spirit realm.

If we fear Satan, it shows that we have more confidence in what he can do than in what God can do to resist him. That type of fear not only gives him an open door; it draws him to you.

REJECT THE SPIRIT OF FEAR

I must confess that I was, for years, tormented by a spirit of fear. I was afraid of everything. That same fear had been on my mother since the night, as a small child, she had heard a man calling for help after he was thrown out of an upstairs window. He apparently cried out most of the night before someone found him.

As a result, Mother was even afraid to go to school the next day. Her father indulged her, and she told me that she remembered lying on the back seat of his car and reading all day as he went about taking care of his business.

As I was growing up, Mother talked fear. "I'm afraid of ..." "I'm worried about ..." "I'm afraid _____ will happen." It just seemed to be part of her normal conversation. When I would hear her say those things, it didn't dawn on me that fear was contagious, just as faith is. Slowly, but surely, I took on her fears, and later I had to be delivered from that bondage.

It was something I fought for years. Each time a new

situation arose, new fears would arise. Each time I had to make a firm decision that I would not back down.

I clearly remember that one day, right before my first husband died, I got down on my hands and knees on the floor and said to God, "I will not get up until You deliver me from this terrible fear." I was there crying out to God for about five hours. Then, suddenly, it was gone, and I felt as free as if nothing had ever happened.

Deliverance is not always freedom from some ugly, horrible secret thing. Most of the things we need deliverance from are as common as fear, anger, sadness, grief and regret. These are the things that plague the Body of Christ everywhere.

And, if the truth were known, the big ugly things are sometimes easier to get rid of than are some of these inner struggles that have become so much a part of our souls and that we regularly act out in our lives.

We need deliverance from fear if we are to minister deliverance to others. There are many wonderful things to be seen in this regard in the account of Satan accusing Job before God:

> *Again there was a day when the sons of God came to present themselves before the LORD, and Satan came also among them to present himself before the LORD. And the LORD said to Satan, "From where do you come?"*
>
> *Satan answered the LORD and said, "From going to and fro on the earth, and from walking back and forth on it."*
>
> *Then the LORD said to Satan, "Have you considered My servant Job, that there is none like him on the earth, a blameless and upright man, one who fears God and shuns evil? And still he holds fast to his integrity,*

155

although you incited Me against him, to destroy him without cause."

So Satan answered the LORD and said, "Skin for skin! Yes, all that a man has he will give for his life. But stretch out Your hand now, and touch his bone and his flesh, and he will surely curse You to Your face!"

And the LORD said to Satan, "Behold, he is in your hand, but spare his life." Job 2:1-6

First, who is presenting himself before whom? Did God bow to Satan? Never! On the contrary, Satan had to bow to God. And in the entire conversation, was there any doubt about who was in charge? I don't think so. Satan could not touch Job without God's permission.

Why is it that we take for granted that Satan is in charge of things? He can only do so much, and whatever he does is not for our benefit. Every battle we have with him is pre-approved by God, and God's intent is that our faith grow and that we be victorious.

God didn't allow Satan to destroy Job, and he won't let him destroy you either. So when the enemy is attacking you, ask God what He wants you to learn from it, what He wants you to do and what His intended outcome is. I am convinced that we don't do this nearly as often as we should.

Satan has a way of making us think that our problems are larger than life, but he is a liar. God is in charge. Our Creator is in control. He's got the whole world in His hands. Anything Satan wants to do in our lives, he has to get God's permission to do.

God is able not only to save us from Hell; He also has made provision for us to have a beautiful and abundant life down here, living as more than conquerors. He will not allow Satan to "chew us up and spit us out."

This great God loves us with an everlasting love, and while we were still in sin, He sent His only begotten Son to die for us, so that we might have eternal life. What a great Gospel!

If the devil has no power with God, what power does he have? Jesus called him *"the ruler of this world"*:

> *"Now is the judgment of this world; now the ruler of this world will be cast out."*   John 12:31

Thank God we are not of this world, so Satan has no power over us. If we are not convinced of that fact, we need to have our minds transformed:

> *And do not be conformed to this world, but be transformed by the renewing of your mind, that you may prove what is that good and acceptable and perfect will of God.*
> Romans 12:2

We are not of this world; we are just passing through. We have a better place to which we are going. This knowledge allows us to *"run and not be weary"* and to *"walk and not faint"* (Isaiah 40:31). Pray for freedom from all fear.

FACE THE ENEMY SQUARELY

> *Therefore take up the whole armor of God, that you may be able to withstand in the evil day, and having done all, to stand.*
> *Stand therefore, having girded your waist with truth, having put on the breastplate of righteousness, and having shod your feet with the preparation of the gospel of peace; above all, taking the shield of faith with which you will be able to quench all the fiery darts of the wicked one. And take the helmet of salvation, and the sword of*

157

the Spirit, which is the word of God; praying always with all prayer and supplication in the Spirit, being watchful to this end with all perseverance and supplication for all the saints. Ephesians 6:13-18

"The full armor of God" refers to battle gear. Get your battle gear on because it is time to go to the front. Stop turning your back to the enemy. It's time to face him.

We must gird our loins with truth, and Jesus is the truth. We are to have our feet shod with the Gospel, and this is the good news of Jesus Christ. We are to put on the breastplate of righteousness, and Jesus is our righteousness. We are to put on the helmet of salvation, and He is our salvation. We are to take the shield of faith, and He is our faith. We are to take the sword of the Spirit, and He is our sword. So, essentially what is being said is that we need to put on Jesus. He is our armor. Let's put Him on.

This is not something automatic for every believer. Paul said we have to put it on. This is what will make us stand. So, stand, and don't ever back down.

DON'T LET YOUR PRAYERS BE HINDERED

We have spoken of things that hinder our prayers and our anointing. As we have seen, unforgiveness is one of those killers:

"And whenever you stand praying, if you have anything against anyone, forgive him, that your Father in heaven may also forgive you your trespasses." Mark 11:25

Unforgiveness is one of the greatest hindrances to our prayers for healing for ourselves or for others. Walk in forgiveness, and you will enjoy better health and your prayers for others will be more effective.

We must keep our hearts free of any known sin. David sang:

> *If I regard iniquity in my heart,*
> *The Lord will not hear.*   Psalm 66:18

What a powerful statement! Sin is a hindrance to our prayers. I'm not just talking about murder, unfaithfulness to a spouse or some of the other things we consider to be big sins. This includes such things as anger, jealousy and greed, and most of us have been guilty of these sins. Harboring anger, jealously or greed in your heart will keep you from being healed, and it will also hinder your prayers for others.

Soon after I became a widow, I was very upset one day with the actions of a person I felt was treating me unfairly in a business transaction. I grew so agitated with this person that I could physically feel the anger rising in me as I drove home that day. God spoke to me and said, "You'd better get rid of that, or it will do you real harm."

I heard what the Lord said, but there was no way I was going to release my anger so quickly and easily. I was mad, and I was determined to stay mad for a while. Before twenty-four hours had passed, I was sick, and I knew that I had brought it on myself.

When I realized what was happening, it didn't take me long to get on my knees and repent and forgive the person who had wronged me. Still, it took me several days to get over the sickness I had brought on myself because of my foolish anger.

It is not necessary to publicly confess every infraction.

159

I'm telling you about my sin so that you can avoid doing the same. Don't be like the Pharisees of whom Jesus spoke:

> *"Woe to you, scribes and Pharisees, hypocrites! For you are like whitewashed tombs which indeed appear beautiful outwardly, but inside are full of dead men's bones and all uncleanness. Even so you also outwardly appear righteous to men, but inside you are full of hypocrisy and lawlessness."* Matthew 23:27-28

God is looking for those who will be so concerned about maintaining a good relationship with Him that they will be careful of their walk, not just of their talk. When He finds them, they will be empowered to minister to others and see them healed.

NEVER ENTERTAIN UNFORGIVENESS

We wonder sometimes how we can forgive and forget. We may never forget, but we must forgive if we expect to have favor with God.

That doesn't mean that we like what has been done to us. Still, we can release it to Him and not keep it in our spirits, where it can do much harm. That thing will keep you in bondage, and it will prevent God from ministering to the person who has done you wrong. By our unwillingness to forgive, we bind our offenders.

We have the keys of the Kingdom, and we must not use them to lock people out. When you do this, those people can't change. You have effectively allowed the enemy an entrance into their lives. What you want to see in them cannot happen until you release them. When we have gone as far as we know to go and done as much as we know to do, often what remains is to release people from guilt because of hurts and offenses of the past.

At one particular point in my own life, I kept trying to rectify a situation with another person, to straighten it out any way I could. But the more I tried to correct the situation, the worse it got. Feeling desperate about it one day, I decided that I would request prayer at a conference I was going to attend.

The speaker at the conference was a lady who had been in a full body cast for years until she was able to take hold of a healing word for her life. Then she was delivered. Since that time she had been ministering healing to others, and she had a very dynamic ministry. I was looking forward to receiving her prayers.

I was disappointed when there were so many sick people to be prayed for that day that the speaker could not get to all of them. She asked us to form into small groups of four or five and to pray for each other.

The people in my group all seemed to be new to that type of thing, so it fell to me to do the praying. This was a disappointment. I had so hoped to find help for that nagging situation, and now I had to pray for everyone else.

No sooner had I finished praying for the needs of the other people in my group than it was time to dismiss the meeting because another workshop was due to begin in the sanctuary. As I was leaving the building, one of the ladies in my group ran after me. She said, "I'm a Presbyterian pastor's wife, and I don't believe in this kind of thing, but the Lord said to tell you this: 'You shall not bow down to them anymore.' " And then she was gone.

I pondered those words on my way out. "You shall not bow down to them anymore." The Lord seemed to be saying that He was giving me liberty to release the matter to Him and let Him take care of it. I went on my way that day with wonderful liberty and assurance that the situation would indeed be resolved and that I could stop struggling with it.

As husbands and wives, we often fail to walk in forgiveness, and the Scriptures tell us that this will hinder our prayers:

> *Husbands, likewise, dwell with them with understanding, giving honor to the wife, as to the weaker vessel, and as being heirs together of the grace of life, that your prayers may not be hindered.*   1 Peter 3:7

Most of us have learned this lesson the hard way. Many conflicts arise in marriage, and if we don't learn to deal with them in a peaceable way, life can become unbearable. When this happens, what was meant to be a foretaste of Heaven on earth can, instead, become a Hell on earth.

KEEP YOUR SLATE CLEAN

Make sure as you're interceding for others that there is nothing in you that can get in the way. When you're praying for others, keep your own slate clean. Confess anything you need to confess before you get started. For the most part, do it in your own prayer time.

It usually isn't wise for us to air our dirty laundry in public, because there are always people present who are not mature enough to handle that. They would be offended. Only share your intimate things with those you know you can trust in this regard. Even some of those whom you consider to be your very best friends can sometimes betray you and use their knowledge of your weaknesses against you. So be very careful in this area.

THE ROLE OF INTERCESSORY PRAYER IN HEALING

PRAY GOD'S WILL

Jesus taught us to pray:

Your will be done
On earth as it is in heaven.   Matthew 6:10

I pray that prayer a lot, and I encourage others to do the same. When I'm praying for something and I'm not exactly sure how to pray, I say, "Lord, Your will." How can I ask for something specific when I'm not sure what God wants in that situation? My prayer might vacillate with my feelings or my understanding of what is involved. I sometimes think that one thing should be done, and in the end, I find that it's something altogether different.

When we pray, "Lord, Your will be done in this situation," we are using the law of binding and loosing in a positive way. We're giving God the opportunity to decide what is best for that situation.

KNOW THAT YOU ARE NEVER ALONE

God is omnipotent, or all-powerful. He's omnipresent, or always present. He's omniscient, or all-knowing. And the wonderful thing is that He never leaves us:

For He Himself has said, "I will never leave you nor forsake you."
So we may boldly say:
"The LORD is my helper;
I will not fear.
What can man do to me?"   Hebrews 13:5-6

163

The Children's Bread

Cast off all fear of ever being abandoned, of ever being alone. You will never be alone, for He is with you. People may abandon us, but God has promised that He won't. He said He would never leave us orphans:

> *"I will not leave you orphans; I will come to you."*
> John 14:18

We have been grafted into the true Vine, and we are now part of the family of God. Nothing can change that. God will never forsake you. Reject that lie from the pit of Hell.

You are cherished by God. You are loved. You are precious in His sight. You are a sweet fragrance in His nostrils. You are an integral part of His family. You are secure in His love — for eternity.

The Role of Fasting in Prayer

We are still flesh and blood, and sometimes we have bad days. We get angry and say things we shouldn't say. We still require some fasting and prayer and a lot of waiting on God to prepare us for being His representatives on the earth.

Fasting should always bring you into a closer relationship with the Lord Jesus Christ, but some fast only to be fasting. It doesn't change them in any way. They are no closer to Jesus when they finish several days of fasting than they were when they began. Let your fast be one of holiness.

Some people need a different kind of fast. They need to fast watching television for some days or a week, so that they can have time to spend with the Lord. Do whatever you need to do to get through to the throne room of God.

Be Patient With Others, As God Has Been Patient With You

Some children are slow to begin to walk or talk, but we don't abandon them. Some children don't do as well in school as others, but we don't abandon them. Some talk early and some talk late, but they are still our children, and we love them. Just as God is patient with you, be patient with other members of the Body of Christ and allow them time to develop to their true capacity. Some mature quickly, and others mature much more slowly, but they all are God's children.

Praying With Those Who Need Christ

Paul's teachings to the Corinthians show us that those who don't yet know Jesus are blinded to the truth:

> *But even if our gospel is veiled, it is veiled to those who are perishing, whose minds the god of this age has blinded, who do not believe, lest the light of the gospel of the glory of Christ, who is the image of God, should shine on them.* 2 Corinthians 4:3-4

Sometimes we can pray and pray and pray for our lost loved ones and see very little results. In these cases, it is often best to release them to God and pray in the Spirit. He knows what the impediment is; He knows what will reach them. Let Him do the work. Often the problem is that their eyes have been blinded; there is a veil over their eyes. We must pray that this blindness be removed.

People may seem to be so dense about spiritual things that we wonder if they will ever change, but once that veil, that mind-blinding spirit that has kept them from truth, is

165

removed they are set free, and they suddenly become totally different persons. Recently, I had a dream about the veil being removed, and I am more convinced than ever that we can pray this prayer for our family members.

Say to the Lord, "I pray right now, in Jesus' name, that the mind-blinding spirit that prevents this loved one from recognizing and accepting the truth will be bound and that he [or she] will come to the saving knowledge of the Lord Jesus Christ. Let him [or her] be snatched out of darkness and brought into Your glorious light." God hears prayers like that.

If we only had a greater understanding of what Hell is like, we would be interceding for more people not to go there — even for those we don't much care for. We would not want anyone to spend eternity there. We can ask God to give us a picture of it to make us understand better.

God has given to us *"the keys of the kingdom"*:

> *"And I will give you the keys of the kingdom of heaven, and whatever you bind on earth will be bound in heaven, and whatever you loose on earth will be loosed in heaven."* Matthew 16:19

He has made our word count:

> *"Again I say to you that if two of you agree on earth concerning anything that they ask, it will be done for them by My Father in heaven. For where two or three are gathered together in My name, I am there in the midst of them."* Matthew 18:19-20

Our power to bind and loose is important. Whatever we bind on earth is bound in Heaven, and whatever we loose on earth is loosed in Heaven. We are often our own worst enemies, because we bind the wrong things and loose the wrong things. I am convinced that these terms relate more than anything else to forgiving and not forgiving. One thing is sure: We haven't yet recognized the extent of the power and authority we have.

The Lord tells us to forgive, and when we fail to forgive, we are binding the situation and preventing God from intervening. We lock people out of God's blessing, and we lock ourselves out with them.

If we forgive, He forgives; and if we don't forgive, He won't forgive. Don't be guilty of this sin, because unforgiveness will bind you and the other person involved. Don't give place to the enemy, as we do so many times. Whatever we bind is bound, and whatever we loose is loosed. We have the keys.

What are you binding today in your life? Take the keys out of your pocket and unlock that thing. What do you need to loose that you're not loosing? When you let go, it will come forth.

God said, *"They will recover."* But for goodness sake, open the door and give someone an opportunity to be set free.

We cannot emphasize too much the need for those to whom we minister healing to become children of God, to know Jesus as Lord and Savior. If someone in your family does not know Him, that prayer request has to be high up on your list for intercessory prayer. Believe God for that mind-blinding spirit to be removed so that person can come to the knowledge of Christ and know where he or she will spend eternity.

Physical healing is important because God wants us to be strong as we walk through life down here. But the greatest healing is that of the spirit, and nothing could be more important.

The Children's Bread

Praying With Those Who Are Approaching Death

It has been my privilege to stand at the bedside of many saints as they were passing into the presence of God. Sometimes they seemed much too young to die, and I wondered if it was truly God's plan to take them in that moment. But He always knows best, and we must leave these decisions with Him.

As people feel death nearing, they often begin to drift into a deep sleep. If we were to prolong their lives at those times, we would only be prolonging their suffering. I pray for God's will to be done and for the proper words to say to them in their dying moments. Often I have said simply, "I'm going to be right here standing guard beside you. You must rest." They often seem to be so very tired of trying to hold on to life that they welcome these words. Sometimes God will surprise us.

On one occasion, Bud and I visited a Veteran's Administration hospital to pray for a man who was in a coma. All of his family members had flown in because doctors had not given him much hope of living. I sat on the side of the bed as we prayed, and the man never moved during the entire time.

After we had gone, however, he woke up. "Where's that woman in the red coat?" he asked, showing that he had been aware of my presence in the room. He got up, greeted everyone and went down to the cafeteria and had dinner with the entire family.

After dinner, they all said their good-byes and went their way. The man went back upstairs and got into bed; before long, he died. What wonderful grace God had given him to be able to say good-bye to all of his family members!

The evening my mother died, I was staying with her.

She said to me, "I feel very funny. Would you mind holding my hand?"

"Of course not," I said.

"Do you love me?" she asked.

I said, "Mom, you know I love you."

"I know you love me," she said, "because you wouldn't do so much for me if you didn't."

Later she said she was feeling better and had decided to go to bed. "Are you going to go to bed, too?" she asked.

"No," I told her. "I'm going to wait for Bud, but I'll be here if you need me. Just call."

Mom had been in her room for only a few minutes when I heard her call, "Lanie!"

"What is it, Mother?" I asked.

"I feel strange again," she said.

"What do you feel?" I asked.

"I don't know," she responded. "I've never felt this way before."

"Okay," I said, "let's pray," and I knelt down beside her, and we prayed together, holding hands.

"I'm all right now," she said. "You can go."

"I'll be in the next room," I told her, "in case you need me during the night."

Before long Mom called me again, and I went into her room. "What is it?" I asked.

"I don't know," she said as before. "I feel strange again. I've never felt this way."

"Do you have pain?" I asked.

"No, I don't have any pain."

"Is it your heart?"

"No, nothing hurts me."

I said, "Mother, I'll tell you what. You pray this time."

She said, "All right." She held her frail hand up to Heaven and prayed a sweet and simple prayer: "Dear

169

Heavenly Father, take me to a safe place to sleep tonight." An hour later, Mother went home to be with Jesus. As her body began to turn cold, I knew that she had gone immediately into His presence.

NEVER DESPISE TIMES OF PREPARATION

Before I got into ministry, I spent years in preparation for it. The teachers in our Bible school told us students that our time in the school was just a beginning. When we got out, we would need to continue living a life of prayer and meditation on God's Word so that when a door of ministry did open for us, we would be ready. That's just what happened, and many of my fellow students are now in powerful ministries in many parts of the world.

I had been studying the Scriptures before going to Bible school, and now I continued to study them. I have stacks of spiral notebooks that I filled with things the Lord revealed to me. He would awaken me during the night and show me something, so I kept my notebooks beside my bed. It was not unusual for me to write fifteen pages or more of notes each night.

I did lie down for a nap in the afternoons when I could, and when I did, the Lord would bring back to me the scriptures I had been studying, almost like a movie. In this way, He would have me review what I had been learning. If we seek Him, we will find Him:

Blessed are those who keep His testimonies,
Who seek Him with the whole heart!   Psalm 119:2

Our problem is that we grow weary and stop seeking God. I cannot emphasize it too much: Don't give up. This is what we tell those who come to the Healing Rooms for prayer, and the same message is for those who are preparing for ministry. Don't give up, and don't back down. Stand firm, and keep seeking God until He opens a door of ministry to you.

For those who go to Bible school or seminary, that's good, but it doesn't mean that you have arrived. It is only a beginning. The Christian life is a present-moment experience. Start walking in the light, and keep walking in the light.

UNDERSTAND THE PURPOSE OF OUR WILDERNESS EXPERIENCES

When any of us goes through a trial, our faith is tested. This is our wilderness experience, and the purpose of it is so that we come forth filled with the Spirit, as Jesus did. His wilderness experience came shortly after He was baptized in water, and it was extremely severe. Still, He came through that trial with even more power, and this is God's plan for our times of testing.

When God allows us to go through something, His intention is that we learn and grow from the experience and come out of it with more power. It was after this experience that Jesus began His ministry, and God wants you and me to receive power through our wilderness experiences that we, too, can impart to others.

NEVER BE OFFENDED OR DISCOURAGED

Just as those who come for healing do, too often those of us who pray become offended or discouraged and stop believing God. Naaman of the Bible was a military commander. When he got leprosy, he was sent to Elisha for help. The prophet told him to go and dip himself in the Jordan River seven times.

171

THE CHILDREN'S BREAD

Naaman was offended by that. He wondered, *Who does he think he is? Doesn't he see my fine clothes.* He asked the prophet, "Isn't there a better river, a cleaner one, that I could dip in?"

But Naaman's servants were wise and said to their master, "If he had told you to do something difficult, you would have done it. So, don't miss it now just because you don't understand it."

Naaman took this sound advice and went to dip in the Jordan, and he was healed. Pride can rob us of our blessings and even keep us out of the Kingdom. We think we know how things ought to be done and how we ought to be treated, but we just need to stop for a minute and ask God to show us what He wants.

These are truths that we must teach to those who come to us for healing, but we must also practice them.

HAVE A HEALTHY FEAR OF GOD

"The fear of the LORD is the beginning of wisdom."
                                                        Proverbs 9:10

All of us need more wisdom, more understanding, and it all starts with a healthy fear of God and respect for His will for our lives.

The fear of the LORD is the beginning of wisdom;
A good understanding have all those who do His commandments.   Psalm 111:10

When we follow God's principles, He will give us good understanding. Learn His Word and obey it. The phrase, "not my will, but Yours be done," is not just a group of pretty words. It is a prayer that will turn your life upside down.

172

Don't Be Afraid to Submit to God

Therefore submit to God. Resist the devil and he will flee from you. James 4:7

First there is the submission to God, and then we have power to resist the enemy and make him flee. As we come under God's covering, we have power to make the devil run away from us.

Get under God's umbrella where you'll be safe, and you will have power over the evil one.

In Everything, Be Guided by God's Word

When you pray, be guided by God's Word. Use it in your prayers. It is anointed, and when you speak it, what you are speaking is anointed. It is powerful, so use its power.

When you speak out the Word, believe it. Sometimes when we want to accomplish grand things, we come up with grand prayers. But our words, however eloquent, are not nearly as powerful as God's words. Use them. You will never discover any more powerful truths than those declared in the Holy Bible.

"For as the rain comes down, and the snow from heaven,
And do not return there,
But water the earth,
And make it bring forth and bud,
That it may give seed to the sower
And bread to the eater,
So shall My word be that goes forth from My mouth;
It shall not return to Me void,
But it shall accomplish what I please,
And it shall prosper in the thing for which I sent it."
Isaiah 55:10-11

173

What does this say about God's Word? It *"shall not return void."* It *"shall accomplish what"* God pleases. It *"shall prosper in the thing for which"* God sent it. Wow! Those are powerful promises.

You can speak God's Word and know that what you are saying is not in vain. You can speak it and know that it will be accomplished. You can speak it and know that it will prosper. Then, why would we not do this? We can say, "God said it, I believe it, and that settles it! Amen!"

God has promised us that He will work with us confirming His Word:

> *And they went out and preached everywhere, the Lord working with them and confirming the word through the accompanying signs. Amen.*　　Mark 16:20

They preached, and the Lord sent the confirmation. There was no other requirement. As they spoke the Word, God would reveal His power to prove it, and there was absolutely nothing Satan could do about it. Believe it and receive it.

> *And take the helmet of salvation, and the sword of the Spirit, which is the word of God.*　　Ephesians 6:17

The Word is our sword, so we must become proficient in using it. You won't be able to wield it perfectly the first time or the second, but if you continually practice using it, you will, in time, become a powerful swordsman.

Hide the promises of God in your heart. Memorize them. There is no other way. As we have seen, King David said:

> *Your word I have hidden in my heart,*
> *That I might not sin against You.*　　Psalm 119:11

When the enemy comes against us like a flood, we are able to raise up this standard against him. God is true, and His Word stands true forever. Settle that in your spirit.

MEDITATE ON GOD'S WORD

God's Word is rich and deep. You will never in this world exhaust its treasures. Begin to plumb its depths more fully. Meditate on it as you pray. Think about it. Ask God to open it up to you. You will be amazed by what He will show you.

I am constantly receiving little tidbits from the Lord, and I share them with my husband. I ask the Lord things, and He answers me.

Search the Scriptures:

> *Then the brethren immediately sent Paul and Silas away by night to Berea. When they arrived, they went into the synagogue of the Jews. These were more fair-minded than those in Thessalonica, in that they received the word with all readiness, and searched the Scriptures daily to find out whether these things were so. Therefore many of them believed, and also not a few of the Greeks, prominent women as well as men.* Acts 17:10-12

The people of Berea searched the Scriptures daily, and that is a good recommendation for all of us. By *"searched"* we mean that they didn't just take it for granted, they didn't just accept everything they were told. They searched it out to know the truth of what they were being taught.

When you hear someone say something you don't understand, write it down for further study. When you read something you don't understand, make a note of it and check to see what you can find about that subject later on.

The Children's Bread

People can say all kinds of things, and we need to know what to receive and what to reject.

Check it out for yourself. Ask the Holy Spirit to bring you understanding of the subject. John wrote:

> *But if we walk in the light as He is in the light, we have*
> *fellowship with one another, and the blood of Jesus Christ*
> *His Son cleanses us from all sin.* 1 John 1:7

What does it mean for us to *"walk in the light"*? I believe it means that we walk in obedience to the revelation we have through the Word of God.

Use Your God-Given Authority

Paul and Barnabas said:

> *"Believe on the Lord Jesus Christ, and you will be saved,*
> *you and your household."* Acts 16:31

We have a certain authority over our own households. Believe for it, and put it to use.

This type of authority doesn't refer to the person in the household who speaks the loudest. Most of us have made that mistake at one time or another, and it just turns people off. Use your authority in prayer. Claim the Word over your household, and watch that household come together in the Lord.

Always Expect an Answer to Your Prayers

Always expect profit from your prayers. Don't pray if you don't expect something to happen. If you do that, you're just wasting your time and everybody else's.

Some people pray such complicated prayers that we have to wonder if they even know what they're saying themselves. Whatever you pray, expect something to happen. When I pray, I mean it, and I believe for things to start happening. If not, I wouldn't bother praying. If I had nothing to say, nothing to claim, I would remain silent. If God told me to pray, then I expect Him to move when I do pray.

Blessing, increase, follows obedience. God is the God of increase.

> *"Therefore I say to you, whatever things you ask when you pray, believe that you receive them, and you will have them."* Mark 11:24

Faith is expectancy. *"Believe ... , and you will have them."* What are you believing for? If you are believing negatively, you will receive negatively. But if you are believing positively, you will receive positively.

There are many things that we believe in a general sense, but not on a personal level. Most of us believe that Jesus died on the cross and that His sacrifice provided us all that we need for godly living in this world, but our problem is believing that He wants to do something about the problem we are having this moment. We have no problem believing that He created the worlds, but we're not sure that He can handle our present situation — or perhaps we're not sure that He really wants to. We must believe that when we pray, God will move on our behalf, that He has all things in His hands and that He is in charge.

Most of us believe that one day we will live with God in Heaven and that it will be wonderful, but our problem is believing for today and what we are experiencing right now. Yet He said that He had come to give us life more abundantly. Was all that He did on Calvary a preparation for Heaven? Of course not. He took the stripes on His back for our healing, and there will be no sickness in Heaven. Healing is only for now, not for Heaven. He took our sadnesses, our griefs, but there will be none in Heaven. That was for the here and now, not for Heaven.

We need healing here and now, not in Heaven. We need comfort and consolation here and now, not when we get to Heaven. We will have eternal life in Heaven, but we can also have a more abundant life right here and right now.

We are in God's Kingdom now, and we need to start walking the Kingdom walk and talking the Kingdom talk. In Heaven, we won't have to worry about prosperity. It is now, here on earth, that we require funds to spread God's Kingdom. Then we won't need them. You need answers to your prayers NOW, and God wants to give you those answers. Believe Him for it.

KNOW THE POWER OF YOUR WORDS

Watch what you say, because words have power in them, to create or to destroy. In the beginning, God was brooding over the void, but nothing happened until He spoke.

Because we are created in God's image, our words also create. What we speak will come forth. If you continue to speak in a negative way, you will bring forth negative things. Don't let the enemy make your tongue his chosen weapon. Yield your tongue to God.

This is why you need to make a Holy Ghost confession about what's going on. Believe that when you pray you receive what He has for you. Believe it when you pray. Say, "Lord, this is what Your Word says. I believe it." Sometimes you have to add, "Help my unbelief."

Next, I want to give you some practical suggestions for enhancing your healing ministry.

178

CHAPTER SIX

PRACTICAL SUGGESTIONS
FOR THE HEALING MINISTRY

There are a number of very practical things we can learn that will help us to be more effective in our ministry of healing to others.

ON THE IMPORTANCE OF UNITY AMONG
THE MEMBERS OF A MINISTRY TEAM

One of the things we need to believe for in the healing ministry is unity among those who minister. Jesus said:

> *"Every kingdom divided against itself is brought to desolation, and every city or house divided against itself will not stand."*   Matthew 12:25

Unity among believers is never an easy thing to maintain, but we must believe for it. In our Healing Rooms, we have lists of prayer needs that we share with our intercessors on a weekly basis, and the need for unity is always on that list. Disunity opens the door to Satan, and he will surely take advantage of it.

When we recognize that God is in charge of this ministry, and each of us submits to Him, there will be a common unity. If each of us wants to be in charge, there can be no unity at all. Nothing delights Satan more than to see us bickering over who has authority in a given situation.

When dealing with sickness, we cannot afford to open doors to him. This is a matter of life and death. Disunity also opens our workers and their families to sickness, and we cannot afford to do that.

How can we maintain unity when working with so many people of such varied temperaments and such varied backgrounds and experiences? How can we maintain unity when we are sure to have disagreements? We must look to the Scriptures.

The men and women of the Bible also had disagreements, but they still found ways to walk together in unity. If even they could not agree on everything, we will certainly never agree on everything. Sometimes we have to agree to disagree, and at the same time, we must recognize that those who are in charge are in charge.

We make sure that our team members know before entering the healing rooms who their team leader is, and who will be taking the lead in the ministry that is performed. Everyone else is to follow the lead of that person.

One of the other members of the team may have a very different idea about how the healing ministry should proceed in that particular case, but because there is a leader in charge, that leader will make this decision, and the others will be expected to follow. Anything else would result in chaos. It is impossible to drive in two directions at the same time, so don't try it.

Those who have a different idea about how the ministry should proceed may just need to wait a while until they can have their opportunity. Let someone else finish what he or she is doing, and then your turn may come.

Whatever you do, don't contradict what someone else is doing at the moment. Sick people don't need more confusion brought upon them, and we don't need confusion disturbing our prayers.

Don't be so busy seeking your own answer to the problem that you fail to back others who have already heard from God in the matter. You back them, and then they will back you.

We make sure going in that all those who participate in our Healing Rooms ministry understand several principles:

- That there is only one leader in each case
- That we must perform our ministry in an orderly way
- That the other members of the team will follow the leader, the person in charge

The person in charge is not always the same in each case. The members of our teams take turns leading. But there is only one leader at any given time.

When one of the teams goes into a room for ministry, the first thing they do is to pray over the information sheet the sick person has filled out. Then they decide who will lead the ministry this particular time. We do this by asking who feels he or she has something from the Lord. When a decision has been reached, the others support that person.

This doesn't mean that we agree with every decision that person makes, but it does mean that we have determined to do things in an orderly and unified way. God is both a God of order and a God of peace, and we must honor His desire in this regard.

As you pray daily for unity, remember that your prayers represent a good and important warfare. A disagreement over procedures can sometimes lead to a natural conflict in the flesh, and this is not pleasing to God.

If someone says or does something that I don't particularly agree with, I first stop to wonder if maybe he knows something that I have not yet sensed. Just because I don't understand what is being said or done doesn't necessarily mean that it isn't true and holy. I may be limited on that particular point, not yet having full understanding of it. So, I honor the Lord and the person ministering by backing him up and refraining from argument or strife.

We must never be guilty of fighting each other. Nothing displeases God more. Our enemy is well defined, and it is not the other members of God's family. If we begin to fight each other, we are doing Satan's work for him.

OPPOSITION WITHOUT WORDS:

Opposition to other members of the Body of Christ can sometimes be more subtle than mere words. We may not say a thing, or even do a thing, but the battle is in our spirits. If something is said or done that you don't understand, ask the person later (after the ministry to the sick person is finished) what he or she meant by that. There may be a very sound explanation, or, if not, that person may need to hear something from you. But never do your correcting in the presence of the people to whom you are ministering.

Most of your battle is not with other men, but with evil spirits:

> *For we do not wrestle against flesh and blood, but against principalities, against powers, against the rulers of the darkness of this age, against spiritual hosts of wickedness in the heavenly places.* Ephesians 6:12

Sometimes, when we are having a confrontation with one of our co-workers, we find it hard to understand why we are even having that particular discussion. That's the work of the enemy, to cause you to wrestle with each other instead of against his evil forces. If he can keep you fighting flesh and blood, you won't have time to wrestle with principalities and powers of the air. Walk in submission to one another to avoid this problem.

Our battle is in the heavenlies:

> *For though we walk in the flesh, we do not war according to the flesh. For the weapons of our warfare are not carnal but mighty in God for pulling down strongholds, casting down arguments and every high thing that exalts itself against the knowledge of God, bringing every thought into captivity to the obedience of Christ.*
>
> 2 Corinthians 10:3-5

Identify the right battle and the right battlefield and stay with it. Refuse to get into battles with your brothers and sisters. Know your true enemy.

When I am speaking, I sometimes notice people who, with their body language, are indicating that they don't agree with what I'm saying. This is disrespectful to the Spirit and His anointing and dishonoring to the person who is ministering. If we have a disagreement with what is being said, we can certainly save it for a later time, for some private moment.

God has declared:

> *Touch not mine anointed, and do my prophets no harm.*
>
> Psalm 105:15, KJV

God does not take it lightly when we oppose the people He is using.

A LACK OF COMMUNICATION:

Many of the disagreements in the Body of Christ can be traced to a failure of communication, and an orderly and

183

respectful discussion will often clear the air. Many times, if we understood where a person was coming from, why he was saying what he was saying, we would not be offended by it. We make excuses for members of our own family (because we understand them), but we're not willing to do the same for people we don't know as well. God can enable us to overcome in this area.

Jesus said of Himself:

> *I am Alpha and Omega, the beginning and the ending, saith the Lord, which is, and which was, and which is to come, the Almighty.*   Revelation 1:8, KJV

He has all authority forever, but He is permitting us to use His authority for a specific time and place. He's the Creator, and everything that was made was made for His pleasure. All holiness is His, but He shares it with us. In Him is all wisdom and knowledge. He's the only One who is all-loving. He's the One who is full of humility and grace. If we experience mercy and grace, it is only because of Him.

The Church we serve is His Church, and the Word we preach is His Word. When we begin to think that we are someone important, we must look at the Source of all that we have been loaned. Give honor and glory to the One from whom all things flow, and recognize the levels of authority He has established in order to avoid disunity in the healing ministry.

ON THE VARIOUS METHODS OF MINISTERING HEALING

There are many biblical ways for ministering healing. All of them are valid and useful. Use the approach the Spirit shows you for a particular case.

Practical Suggestions for the Healing Ministry

The Laying On of Hands:

"And these signs will follow those who believe: In My name they will cast out demons; they will speak with new tongues; they will take up serpents; and if they drink anything deadly, it will by no means hurt them; THEY WILL LAY HANDS ON THE SICK, and they will recover." Mark 16:17-18

This is an important procedure for healing, and it is used in conjunction with several of the other means, because there is an actual transference that takes place. Doctors have to lay their hands on people to minister to them, and how much better it is to have anointed hands laid on us when we're sick!

Before you lay hands on someone, make sure that you are anointed and covered by the blood of Jesus. Don't risk opening yourself to sickness coming from the other person. Don't make yourself vulnerable before the enemy. Because you are about to minister healing to that person and overcome the power of the enemy in that life, he will try to attack you. As long as you are covered by the blood and anointed, you have nothing to worry about. We pray for all of those who minister in the Healing Rooms that they will not take home anything with them at the end of the day that is not of our heavenly Father.

Cover your people with the blood of Jesus. Speak the Word of God over them so that when they leave that place, they are cleansed. Cover your family members, too, so that the enemy will not be able to attack them.

Calling for the Elders:

Is anyone among you sick? Let him CALL FOR THE ELDERS OF THE CHURCH, and let them pray over

185

*him, anointing him with oil in the name of the Lord.
And the prayer of faith will save the sick, and the Lord
will raise him up. And if he has committed sins, he will
be forgiven.*

James 5:14-15

Sometimes this method is necessary, and when it is, don't hesitate to use it.

AGREEING TOGETHER:

*"Again I say to you that IF TWO OF YOU AGREE on
earth concerning anything that they ask, it will be done
for them by My Father in heaven. For where two or three
are gathered together in My name, I am there in the midst
of them."*

Matthew 18:19-20

Get someone to agree with you. There is great strength in numbers. The Scriptures teach:

*How could one chase a thousand,
And two put ten thousand to flight,
Unless their Rock had sold them,
And the LORD had surrendered them?*

Deuteronomy 32:30

Having the right person to agree with you, to stand with you and to believe with you, is a wonderful thing. But be careful. Two opposites cancel each other out, so don't risk "agreeing" with the wrong person.

For example, one might pray, "By the stripes on Jesus' back, you've been healed," and another might respond, "Well, I hope so." These words would effectively cancel out the positive prayer. We need prayers of agreement from people of agreement.

Practical Suggestions for the Healing Ministry

Having Whatever You Ask:

"And in that day you will ask Me nothing. Most assuredly, I say to you, WHATEVER YOU ASK the Father in My name He will give you. Until now you have asked nothing in My name. ASK, AND YOU WILL RECEIVE, that your joy may be full." John 16:23-24

I like this promise. *"Whatever you ask* [whatever you need, whatever you are believing for] *... He will give you."* What are we waiting for? Let's claim it.

Speaking the Word:

When evening had come, they brought to Him many who were demon-possessed. And He cast out the spirits with a word, and healed all who were sick, that it might be fulfilled which was spoken by Isaiah the prophet, saying:
"He Himself took our infirmities
And bore our sicknesses." Matthew 8:16-17

Jesus *"cast out the spirits with a word."* Speak the Word over the sick and get them healed. Sick people can also read the promises in the Word of God themselves, speak them and be healed.

Those who become part of the Healing Rooms ministries receive a list of healing Scriptures I have compiled. It contains promises of healing for salvation, relationships, inner healing, practical needs, finances, physical healing for the body and whatever else we need. If the person who is ministering can't think of a particular scripture verse, he or she can look it up in that booklet and read it to those who are in need.

In Old Testament times, rabbis wore tassels on the hems

of their garments, and those tassels represented God's promises. That's why the woman with the issue of blood wanted to touch the hem of Jesus' garment. The Jewish people had confidence in the Word of God and in its power. When she said, "If I can just touch the hem of His garment, I know I'll be healed," she was recognizing Him as a man of God.

She had heard about Him and the many things He was doing. Then she saw the tassel on His garment that represented the Word. If she could just touch it, she was sure, she would be healed. And it was so.

It would be a good idea for anyone going into the healing ministry to get a binder and make a notebook containing all of the Scripture promises regarding healing. Some few have such good memories that they don't need anything written, but most of us need it. By doing this, you are arming yourself with the proper weapons and protecting yourself with proven armor.

CONFESSING OUR SIN:

Confess your trespasses to one another, and pray for one another, THAT YOU MAY BE HEALED. The effective, fervent prayer of a righteous man avails much.

James 5:16

In many ways, I admire the tradition of daily or regular confession. I know that this doctrine is taken to extremes and that those ministering sometimes require impractical acts of penance of those who confess, rather than simply leading them to forgiveness and reconciliation through Jesus. Nevertheless, the idea of coming to God on a daily basis and clearing our souls of anything that would hinder us for that day is an excellent one, and it has benefits that go far beyond those for the soul.

Confession is good, and it is not just for good for the soul. When you're praying for the sick and they wish to confess some sins, let them do it. There is something wonderful about ridding oneself of garbage. That act of purification can go a long way to bring healing to a person's body.

Jesus was sinless, of course, and He did not have things to confess to the Father. Nevertheless, people, who are sinful, were all around Him. They were constantly pulling at Him and seeking things from Him. Even the men who traveled with Him, and thus lived in very close fellowship with Him, were far from perfect, and their failures weighed on Him. He sadly asked them one day:

> *"O faithless generation, how long shall I be with you?*
> *How long shall I bear with you?"*   Mark 9:19

Jesus had struggles, too, just like we do, and He had to develop a way of cleansing Himself from daily cares. If He hadn't, He would have had to carry them around with Him, and before long, He would have been saying, "Tell the people I'm very sorry, but I can't minister today. I have a terrible headache." There is no record of Jesus ever having done that, and it was because He had a way of regularly cleansing His soul.

Those who minister healing must take a lesson from this. If you are to help others overcome their physical problems, you must walk so close to Jesus that you are personally kept. You cannot be heavy laden yourself, or you will not be able to bring healing to others.

Before we allow anyone to go into the rooms for ministry to others, we pray over them and anoint them with oil. Some tell us that when they come out of the healing rooms in the afternoon, they are exhausted and must be careful not to carry with them any of the spirits they have dealt with during the day. They have to know that there are no chinks in their personal armor where evil spirits can penetrate. They can't give place to the enemy.

These are all well-proven means for bringing healing. If, however, God shows you something else to do, as He often does, since He has placed *"gifts of healing"* within the Church (see 1 Corinthians 12:9), obey Him.

IT'S NOT IN THE METHOD:

Many people have developed particular methods that they use for healing, and they expect everyone to be healed in the same way. When the Charismatic Movement swept into our city some thirty years ago, I began attending six or seven different meetings each week, and in each meeting, I wrote down carefully the instructions that were given about the proper method for receiving healing. I tried all of them, and still I could not receive healing.

Eventually, I came to the conclusion that my healing would not come through a certain method. I had to take it by faith in the grace of God and His love for me. I had to believe that He had paid the price for it and that it was just waiting for me to claim. That was what worked for me, and God did an amazing thing. Let God decide the particular way He will work in each particular case.

A CAUTION CONCERNING THE LAYING ON OF HANDS

The writer of Hebrews included the laying on of hands as one of the elementary doctrines of the faith, along with baptisms, the resurrection of the dead and eternal judgment (see Hebrews 6:2), so it is important. In the process of the healing ministry, we lay hands on many people, and we must be very practical in our approach to this aspect of the ministry. When women come for prayer, there should always be other women among the ministry team. The men of the team must be very careful about where and how they lay their hands on a woman being prayed for.

The same is true of women laying hands on a man. These are just practical and commonsense precautions we must all take to avoid criticism. Don't risk doing anything that would discredit what God is doing. Be orderly and discreet in all that you do so that no one will be offended.

If a woman has a heart problem and a male minister feels the need of laying hands on her, let one of the women place her hand over the woman's heart first. Then the man can put his hand on top of her hand.

In this litigious society in which we live, there is a second reason for caution. Some people will look for any reason at all to come after God's servants for money. Don't give them an opportunity. I believe in the laying on of hands, and I know how important it is, but I also know that it must be exercised cautiously and discreetly.

A Caution Concerning Signs

We must never allow signs to become more important to us or our ministries than is the Word of God itself. Signs are only for the confirmation of God's promises; they can never replace God's promises. Signs, on their own, are meaningless. Because signs are exciting and they draw crowds, some have been guilty of emphasizing the signs over the truths of God's Word. This is an error of which you and I must never be guilty.

Signs are not an end in themselves. Their only purpose is to draw men to Christ. He is the End-all and Be-all. Men must never follow signs, but rather follow Christ. Sometimes we can be like little children, playing with the things God has given us without even bothering to develop a deeper relationship with the great Giver of all such gifts. It is time to grow up, stop playing around like little children and get serious about the things of God.

It is also important to realize that the presence of signs is never to glorify us as individuals. It is Christ who is to be exalted — always. All honor be unto Him forever and ever.

A CAUTION WITH REGARD TO ISSUES OF DIVORCE AND REMARRIAGE

Many of those seeking physical healing are either divorced or already separated, and they often divulge this in the course of conversation. Don't be guilty of praying for something that clearly isn't the will of God, for instance, that God would provide another spouse. A person may feel that another spouse is what he or she needs at the moment, but because you are responsible to know the will of God in this regard, never pray against the will of God.

The person may be seeking another spouse, but God may have that one in the present circumstances so that His will can be clearly revealed. God's ideal for marriage is that partners not be cast away so quickly and easily. God desires reconciliation when it is possible.

Sometimes reconciliation is not possible (although all things are possible with God). This is because at least one of the partners is not open to God's will and will not receive it.

Divorce is nothing new. It also existed in Old Testament times, and God said it was *"because of the hardness of [men's] hearts"* (Matthew 8:19). This is not to put anyone down, but we know that the perfect will of God is for restoration, and we know that no case is too difficult for Him. When one or both parties in the marriage are not open to that, there is little God (or anyone else) can do to help them.

We should at least attempt to instill in those who are seeking divorce the vision God inspires of reconciliation, for we are limited only by the size of our vision. When we do not have His vision, in a very real way, we can limit what He will do.

Can God be limited? In one sense, He can't. But He has chosen to work only as men believe and receive. What we do, then, places a very real limit on His activity. He can work only as we believe Him to, so wherever your vision stops, that's where you have unknowingly set the limit.

This is where the promises of the Word of God are so important. We must raise the people's sights. We must enlarge their vision. We must encourage them to go a step beyond, by showing them the perfect will of God in a given situation.

On Bringing Men and Women to Salvation As We Minister Healing

Jesus never healed people just to be healing them. He always had something more important and more eternal in mind. Through the healing of his son, the nobleman and his entire household were saved. This is one of the reasons that healing and the healing ministry are so important. They cause men to believe on Jesus and be saved. This is why God is calling each of us to the healing ministry. Through a single miracle of healing, entire families can be won to Christ.

We know that a person can go to Heaven without being healed, but that same person cannot go to Heaven without being saved. One of the purposes of healing, therefore, is to draw men and women to Christ so that they can be saved.

They may not be seeking Him for that purpose. They may be approaching Him only because He is the Healer, but when He does the miracle they need, they often will believe and be changed.

Many people ask us if we need to make sure the people to whom we are ministering healing are saved first. We must turn to Jesus, our supreme example, for the answer. I don't see Jesus asking the people He ministered to whether or not they were saved before He healed them. He didn't hesitate to pay the price for our healing *"while we were still sinners"*:

> *But God demonstrates His own love toward us, in that while we were still sinners, Christ died for us.*
>
> Romans 5:8

Jesus knew that the demonstration of His love toward us would eventually bring us to salvation, but He didn't demand that we be saved before we received it. Healing is a most wonderful tool for bringing men and women to Christ, so it often comes before salvation.

Some Christians are overzealous in this regard. When they minister to non-Christians or nominal Christians, they make too many demands of them before they have even seen God's miracle-working power. God heals people who have not yet said the sinner's prayer. He heals those who are nominal Christians, and, although it may shock some Christians, He even heals non-Christians. Of course, it is His desire to draw those persons to Himself, but He does it through the demonstration of His love for them, not through discussing doctrinal issues.

When you insist that people believe what you believe before you can pray for them, it sounds like you are only interested in converting them to your way of thinking rather than helping them to be healed. Healing is one of God's most wonderful ways of expressing His love to those who don't know Him; it is not just a reward for correct behavior.

Be merciful in your dealings with the lost; Jesus was. If you are not able to lead that person to the Lord immediately, there will undoubtedly be another opportunity. Let God work it out.

Whatever else you do, always minister in love. Love overcomes every obstacle, and love never fails. Tell the people to whom you minister that God loves them and wants them to be healed. Tell them that you love them and that you want to minister the healing power of God to them. As you express your love in this way, they will open to other things you have to say, and your opportunity to lead them to the feet of Jesus will come more speedily.

"Would you like to receive Jesus?" should be an easy and natural thing to say; it should never be forced. "Well, would you pray for Buddhists?" some ask. Of course, and as I prayed, I would believe that the goodness of God demonstrated through His healing touch would bring them to repentance. I would believe God to give me the opportunity to minister to them in this way.

When we are praying for people's healing, we can be claiming them for the Kingdom. But when people have come for healing, you can't always "blow them out of the water" with your words.

Never have a condemning spirit, because Jesus did not condemn any man. If people feel that you are condemning them, they won't stay around very long. Yes, we want all men to be saved, but there are ways to approach it. John wrote:

And many other signs truly did Jesus in the presence of his disciples, which are not written in this book: but these

195

*are written, that ye might believe that Jesus is the Christ,
the Son of God; and that believing ye might have life
through his name.* John 20:30-31, KJV

Miraculous signs will bring men to Christ as nothing
else will, and healing is one of the important signs He left
us. These signs will cause men to *"believe that Jesus is the
Christ, the Son of God."* So, the believing will often come
after the sign, not before.

We want men to be saved, but we can't force them to be
saved. Repeating a sinner's prayer when they are not ready
for it is not a magic formula that will always bring salvation. Let the Spirit do His work of convicting and wooing
the hearts of men. Be sensitive to His leading, and wait for
your divine opportunity.

I have been to Israel many times, but the very first time
I went, I was not touched with the true need of the Jewish
people. Bud was showing me around Jerusalem one day,
and we came to the Wailing Wall. The Jewish people were
lined up along the wall praying, the men on one side and
the women on the other.

The men all had their prayer books, and they were bow-
ing in petition to God. The women had written their petitions on small pieces of paper, and then they had gone forward to stuff the papers into the cracks in the ancient rocks.
They were now leaning up against the wall praying and
weeping before the Lord.

As we got nearer, Bud nudged me in the back and said,
"Go on down there." I turned to protest, but he was gone.

I couldn't go down to the Wall, could I? But it looked
like I had no other choice.

As I got closer, I noticed that all of the ladies had shawls
on, and when someone handed me one, I put it on, cover-

ing my head as the others had done. I looked to see if there was something else I should do, and it seemed that this was all that was required, so I made my way forward.

When I reached the Wall, I noticed that a lady was seated in a chair facing the Wall. Her face and hands were pressed to the ancient Wall, as she wept and prayed. Then, however, she arose and left, and I took her place.

I sat down in the chair, bowed my head and prayed exactly what I was feeling. My prayer didn't seem to be very spiritual. "Father," I prayed, "I really feel stupid." Believe me, those were the exact words of my prayer. I continued in this helpless way, "And I don't know what to pray."

The Spirit of God spoke to me and said, "Look around you. Pray for them, for they have no Christ to enable them to reach the throne room. Pray for them that I'll answer their prayers."

Oh, what mercy I felt that day! God loves His people. Oh, that we would each one demonstrate that same mercy to others. This includes our own family members. Be more loving to them, and it will be easier to bring them into the Kingdom.

ON MINISTERING THE HOLY SPIRIT BAPTISM AS WE MINISTER HEALING

Another of the things we minister in the Healing Rooms is the baptism of the Holy Spirit. When a believer has not yet received this experience, he lacks power. The baptism with the Holy Spirit is part of what God offers to every believer, and we all need it. We must not be hesitant or afraid to introduce this truth to those who come to us for help. With the power of the Holy Spirit working in us, we are much better able to overcome every evil in this world.

The speaking in tongues that comes to us when we have been baptized in the Spirit is an important element of our prayer life. I pray in the tongues every day because it edifies me. It builds up my spirit. Jude wrote to the early Church:

> *But you, beloved, building yourselves up on your most holy faith, praying in the Holy Spirit ...*   Jude 20

I want my spirit to be stronger than the flesh, so I exercise it. Those who do physical exercises know how this can build up your strength over time. The same is true for the strengthening of the spirit through speaking in tongues. Paul wrote to the Corinthians:

> *He who speaks in a tongue edifies himself.*
> 1 Corinthians 14:4

There are many wonderful teachings on this subject in this chapter of First Corinthians. Those who want to learn more would do well to study that entire section.

Tongues can also come with interpretation as a message from God to our hearts. Some time ago, I began praying one morning, and I quickly realized that my speaking in tongues was not the usual day-to-day speaking in tongues. Bud came in to pray with me, and I said to him, "This is prophetic."

After speaking in tongues for some minutes, the Lord then gave me the interpretation. And what God told us that day consisted of truths that I had not been aware of before. Take any opportunity to help those who come to you for prayer to move into this wonderful experience that will strengthen and expand their lives in the Spirit.

PRACTICAL SUGGESTIONS FOR THE HEALING MINISTRY

WHAT IF THEY DON'T GET HEALED?

The question most everyone asks when we speak of ministering healing to others is: What if we pray and the person doesn't get healed? I know that this is a frightening and embarrassing thought to many, but it need not be. The actual healing is not our responsibility. After all, we can't heal. All we can do is pray and do whatever else the Lord shows us to do. Then, once we have done our part, we have to leave the rest with God.

Christ's sacrifice was accepted by the Father God as payment for sin and its penalty, and that's all we need to know. Jesus said, *"They shall lay hands on the sick, and they shall recover,"* and that's all we need to know. We do what we can do, and the rest is His responsibility.

Now, let us look again at the woman who learned about healing as *The Children's Bread.*

CHAPTER SEVEN

THE CHILDREN'S BREAD

Then Jesus went out from there and departed to the region of Tyre and Sidon. And behold, a woman of Canaan came from that region and cried out to Him, saying, "Have mercy on me, O Lord, Son of David! My daughter is severely demon-possessed."   Matthew 15:21-22

Sometimes we wonder if God is doing anything at all, but He is. He is pulling us into a stronger position of faith. He knows what we're ready for and what we can handle. He will not entrust more harvest into our hands than we can handle. Some people are so joyful when they are healed, only to lose the victory entirely when they are again attacked by the enemy. And he will attack again. God wants to make us strong enough to endure all tests.

Jesus, being a Jew, did not normally minister to the people of Tyre and Sidon. He was not called to their area. But apparently this woman had heard about Him. This shows us how powerful hearing is. It instills faith. People are drawn to places where they hear something is happening, and their faith is stirred because of it. This is why we need to talk and talk and keep on talking, preach and preach and keep on preaching the goodness of the Lord.

THE CHILDREN'S BREAD

The woman cried out to Jesus, *"O Lord, Son of David, my daughter is severely demon possessed."* Oddly enough, Jesus didn't answer her:

> *He answered her not a word.*   Matthew 15:23

Doesn't it seem strange that Jesus didn't say a word to this woman? Or is it strange? Doesn't He do the same to us sometimes? We ask God for something, and we don't hear any answer coming our way. At times, we even begin to wonder what is happening. *Is God out to lunch with the angels? What is going on?*

The disciples seemed to understand Jesus' reticence and even urged Him to send the woman away:

> *And His disciples came and urged Him, saying, "Send her away, for she cries out after us."* Matthew 15:23

Jesus' answer explained His silence:

> *But He answered and said, "I was not sent except to the lost sheep of the house of Israel."* Matthew 15:24

I believe that what Jesus said was not only for the sake of the disciples, but even more so for the sake of the woman. He was challenging her faith. And she responded:

> *Then she came and worshiped Him, saying, "Lord, help me!"*   Matthew 15:25

This woman knew her Source of strength and healing. It was in this moment that Jesus revealed a most wonderful truth about healing:

THE CHILDREN'S BREAD

*But He answered and said, "It is not good to take the
children's bread and throw it to the little dogs."*

Matthew 15:26

An answer like this might well have offended many
people, but not this woman. She was not about to be "put
off." She knew what she needed, she knew where she could
get it and she was determined that nothing would stop
her. This is the spirit of perseverance that all sick people
need to maintain in order to be healed. It sometimes takes
a while to get where you're going, but don't stop until
you're there.

A delay is not a denial. Just because it takes time to get
somewhere doesn't mean that we can't go. There may be
some stops along the way, but keep your eye on the final
destination and know that you will arrive.

The Word of God provides us with a road map that
shows us where we are going, and no matter how many
detours we have to take along the route, we must believe
that we will eventually get where we are going. When anyone begins to get discouraged that this is true, they need to
take another look at the road map, the promise of God's
Word.

Healing is *The Children's Bread*, and if you are one of the
children, it's for you. Jesus could not have made this clearer.

Can you imagine what this woman must have been feeling about then? She was hurting because she had a demon-
possessed child to care for, she had heard about this great
Healer, this Christ, the Man everyone was talking about.
She had made the effort to come to Him, and yet He had
apparently thrown cold water in her face and called her a
"*dog*." For many, that would have been hard to take.

Still, this woman was not discouraged. She knew what

she wanted, and she knew she was in the right place to get it. Her response amazed everyone:

> *And she said, "Yes, Lord, yet even the little dogs eat the crumbs which fall from their masters' table."*
>
> Matthew 15:27

What a wonderful revelation! This is the kind of determination each of us needs to display. This is the attitude that moves the heart of God. Let's grow up and stop being discouraged by every little thing. Let's go back to God again and again and again until the victory comes.

The enemy is counting on the fact that we will get tired and discouraged and stop trying. Let's put him in his place. He is counting on the fact that our pride will prevent us from persevering. *After all, enough is enough. We deserve better*, we think. *Why should we wait for our healing?*

Naaman is a wonderful example of this truth. He was a very important man in Syria, but a great tragedy came into his life. He contracted leprosy, a sickness that would eventually have made him a social outcast. Desperate for healing, and hearing about the many miracles God was doing for His people in Israel, Naaman traveled there, expecting to receive help from the king. The king, however, sent him to the prophet Elisha.

Because of Naaman's position, he was expecting the prophet to give him some special treatment and was amazed when Elisha did not even come to the door to greet him. Rather, he sent a servant to tell him to go to the Jordan River and dip himself in it seven times.

Here was Naaman, decked out in his finest clothes and willing to pay for his healing, and this was the way the prophet chose to treat him. *Who does he think he is?* Naaman must have been thinking. And what was the prophet thinking?

Sometimes God is attempting to remove a person's ego from the situation so that He can be exalted. This is what the woman understood, when she accepted Jesus' words, and this is what Naaman eventually understood. Initially, he was furious, but he did what he was told, dipped seven times in the Jordan and was healed.

When the Canaanite woman responded as she did, she moved the heart of God. Jesus immediately answered her with a most amazing statement:

> *"O woman, great is your faith! Let it be to you as you desire."*
> Matthew 15:28

The miracle the woman was seeking happened:

> *Her daughter was healed from that very hour.*
> Matthew 15:28

We can't take no for an answer, for a no answer is not from God. He may decree a delay, and He may test you by taking you by a circuitous route to your destination, but His ultimate will for you is always "Yes" and "Amen"!

It you are continually hearing "No," that no can't be from God. All noes come from the enemy. He's the one who desires to steal from you, kill you and destroy you. God wants to give you life, and He wants to do it more abundantly. Just be patient:

> *And we desire that each one of you show the same diligence to the full assurance of hope until the end, that you do not become sluggish, but imitate those who*

*THROUGH FAITH AND PATIENCE INHERIT THE
PROMISES.* Hebrews 6:11-12

What was the writer saying? In the dialect of the day, we could say it was, "Hang in there, baby." If we demonstrate *"faith and patience,"* we will *"inherit the promises."* Don't *"become sluggish"* and lose the hope of these promises.

"Patience" is not something any of us like to learn and practice, but patience is easier when we have hope, when we know that God's promises are always *"yea"* and *"Amen,"* when we have a vision of a better tomorrow. Patience bridges the gap between faith and hope, and this is important because many of us are destroyed trying to get from one to the other.

God is maturing us so that we can stand steady in the times of waiting, whether they be short or long, so that we can hold on to what He has promised us until we see it come to pass. Patience helps us to grow spiritual muscles.

If a doctor prescribes a ten-day course of medication for you, and you are still feeling sick at the end of three days, do you then give up and stop taking the medicine? Some people do, but that's not a very wise medical decision. In the same way, we are foolish to give up on God before His "prescription" has a chance to take effect in our lives.

Many people, when they begin to feel better after a few days, discontinue their medication, and the long-term results are not good. Although they are better, their systems are not fully restored to health and they remain vulnerable to other sicknesses or to a relapse into the same sickness. We must do what God prescribes for us and keep on doing it so that we can be healed and maintain good health.

When there is a recurrence of an illness, it is often worse than the original because a more virulent strain of the germ has now developed. Believe God's prescription and follow it carefully so that you can receive your full healing. It is *The Children's Bread.*

Christ Is "Our Passover"

Jesus has completed everything necessary to make us free, and He is waiting for us to make the next move. He was our Passover Lamb:

> *Therefore purge out the old leaven, that you may be a new lump, since you truly are unleavened. For indeed Christ, our Passover, was sacrificed for us.*
>
> 1 Corinthians 5:7

Christ is our Passover, and He was sacrificed for us. He was the sacrificial Lamb. Think about that! God prepared a special Lamb just for you and me. This was no ordinary lamb; this Lamb was without spot or blemish. He chose to die in our stead so that we could partake freely of His sacrifice. The Sinless One took upon Himself our sins. What a Savior!

There is no other sacrifice. Jesus is our Passover, and it is His sacrifice that causes us to pass from death unto life. Believe it and receive it.

We cannot walk in spiritual blindness and expect God's healing to be manifest in our lives, just as we cannot ignore truth and expect to be saved spiritually. Many who call themselves Christians have merely given mental assent to the fact that Jesus is Savior. They have never personally experienced His salvation, never personally received the transfer of His righteousness for their sins. Therefore, they are still walking in spiritual blindness.

After we are genuinely saved, the Word of God contains absolutely everything we need to come into spiritual maturity, and to receive all that God has provided for us through His Son. From then on, it's a matter of how much we are willing to sacrifice to receive it.

There is no substitute for a personal prayer life, a personal knowing and fellowshipping with God. Corporate prayer is good, but it's not enough. Each of us needs to develop our own personal relationship with the Father. When we learn to come to Jesus and to say to Him, "I can't make it without You, and there are situations in my life that require Your constant help," we develop an intimate personal relationship with Him. Then, when we get sick, we will have the necessary assurance that we are His and that we are walking daily in fellowship with Him.

When our relationship with God is not as deep as it should be, the fault is never His. He is not the one who has distanced Himself from us. Rather, we have distanced ourselves from Him.

As we have seen, healing was manifested even in Old Testament times:

And the LORD *listened to Hezekiah and healed the people.*
2 Chronicles 30:20

This particular case happened during the time of Passover. The purpose of Passover being celebrated each year by the Jewish people (then and now) was to remember, to be reminded, of the wonderful deliverance given to the Jews in the time of Moses. We, too, need to be reminded of God's faithfulness, of His ability, of His constancy and of His promises.

When we do something that brings to remembrance the fact that we have been set free, it seems that we are set free all over again. We may not even have understood that there was a bondage growing in our lives, but suddenly we are free again.

If there is no one else around to remind you of what God has done, remind yourself. Speak out the wonderful statements of faith recorded in the Scriptures, and watch as you are released from prisons the enemy has been stealthily building around you.

In Egypt, the Israelites ate the flesh of the Passover lamb, and it gave them physical strength for the journey ahead. What we Christians do in the Communion is very similar. The bread that we partake of represents the body of the Passover Lamb that was broken for us. We take it and eat it, knowing that by His stripes we are healed. He suffered in the flesh so that we might not have to suffer. Through taking His body, we gain strength.

Also in the Communion, we partake of the cup, representing the blood of Jesus that was shed for us for the remission of sins. There is no remission of sins without the shedding of blood, so it was necessary to have a blood sacrifice. That was part of God's plan. Jesus had to die physically for you and me. His blood had to be shed. At the same time, however, He took pain and abuse upon His body for our physical healing. Remind yourself often of what He has done for you.

I love to take Communion and to remember, but I remember more often than each Communion Sunday. I think of Christ's sacrifice as often as I can.

Many modern Christians dread the coming of Communion Sunday. They know they will get out twenty minutes later than usual, and they're afraid that people from other churches will get ahead of them in restaurant waiting lines. Oh, dear one, don't shortchange the Communion experience. This is our life. This is our strength.

Jesus was willing to give His life for fallen creatures like us, and we should be ready to take advantage of every part of His sacrifice. To reject His salvation is to *"put Him to an open shame,"* and we must also not reject the stripes He bore for our healing.

When our children are born, we are amazed to have such precious bundles of love, and our desires for them are great. We would like to give them everything. Yet we have so little to offer. At these times, we must remember Christ's sacrifice. He has provided everything our children and grandchildren need for the future.

What does all of this have to do with the ministry of healing? It has everything to do with it. The entire foundation of the healing ministry rests upon the sacrifice of Christ on Calvary. If we fail to recognize the price that was paid for us, we may have difficulty receiving or ministering healing. If we forget how much love Jesus showed for all mankind on Calvary, we may fail to have sufficient compassion for those who are sick.

As we consider our own physical needs and those of the many sick and suffering around us, we must never lose sight of the provision our Lord has made for us all. It is, after all, *The Children's Bread.*

INDEX OF HEALING SCRIPTURES
USED IN THE BOOK

Ministry address:

Elaine C. Bonn
THE MASTER'S TOUCH MINISTRIES
4385 THIELEN AVENUE
EDINA, MINNESOTA 55436

e-mail: elaineb@usinternet.com